Book 1 - Wealth Management Strategies

Chapter 1: An Introduction to Chartered Wealth Manager (CWM)

What is CWM?

When it comes to managing wealth, there are various certifications and designations one could pursue. However, one that stands out amongst the rest is the Chartered Wealth Manager (CWM) designation. Offered by the American Academy of Financial Management (AAFM), the CWM program is a comprehensive and prestigious certification that equips individuals with the knowledge and skills necessary to excel in the world of wealth management. The CWM designation is recognized globally and is highly sought after by professionals in the financial industry. It covers a wide range of topics including estate planning, tax management, and client relationship management, making it a well-rounded program that prepares individuals for all aspects of wealth management. But why pursue CWM? And what are the benefits of obtaining this designation? Let's explore further.

Why pursue CWM?

First and foremost, pursuing CWM sets you apart from the rest. It shows your dedication and commitment to your profession, as well as your willingness to constantly improve and keep up with the ever-changing world of finance. It also demonstrates your expertise in various areas of wealth management, making you a valuable asset to any organization or client. Furthermore, obtaining the CWM designation allows you to expand your knowledge and skills beyond your current role. In today's competitive job market, having a diverse skill set is crucial in securing and advancing in your career. The CWM program covers a wide range of topics, giving you the opportunity to learn about areas that may not be a part of your current job responsibilities. This not only helps you to become a well-rounded professional, but it also opens up new opportunities for you within the industry. In addition, the CWM program is designed for professionals at all levels, from entry-level to experienced executives. This means that even if you are just starting out in your career, pursuing CWM can give you a head start and set you on the path towards a successful and fulfilling career in wealth management.

Benefits of CWM

One of the key benefits of obtaining the CWM designation is the enhanced credibility it brings. Clients and employers see the CWM designation as a mark of excellence and expertise, giving you a competitive edge in the industry. It also allows you to build trust and establish strong relationships with clients, as they can be assured that their financial needs are being handled by a qualified and knowledgeable professional. Moreover, the CWM program not only covers technical knowledge but also emphasizes ethical standards and values. This ensures that individuals with the CWM designation adhere to high ethical standards in their work, building trust and integrity in the industry. Additionally, the CWM program constantly updates and refreshes its curriculum, ensuring that individuals are equipped with the most up-to-date knowledge and skills in wealth management. This not only benefits the individual, but also their clients and organizations as they receive top-notch service and advice. In a constantly changing and evolving world, staying ahead of the game is crucial. Pursuing the CWM designation ensures that you are up-to-date with the latest trends and strategies in wealth management, making you a valuable asset to any organization or client.

In conclusion, the CWM designation is not just another certification or designation, but a mark of prestige, expertise, and dedication to the field of wealth management. Pursuing CWM not only sets you apart from the rest, but it also opens up new opportunities and allows you to continuously improve and excel in your career.

Chapter 2: Evolution of Wealth Management

Rise of CWM

Wealth management has come a long way from its humble beginnings in ancient times, when wealthy individuals relied on personal advisors to manage their assets. The concept of modern wealth management as a distinct profession began to take shape in the late 19th and early 20th century, with the rise of industrialization and the emergence of large fortunes. However, it wasn't until the 1980s that wealth management truly began to evolve into the sophisticated and dynamic field that we know today. One significant development in the evolution of wealth management was the emergence of the Chartered Wealth Manager (CWM) designation. The CWM is a globally-recognized certification that demonstrates a high level of expertise in wealth management. It was established in 1990 by the American Academy of Financial Management (AAFM), and has since gained recognition and popularity among industry professionals and clients alike.

Impact on Industry

The CWM designation has had a profound impact on the wealth management industry, raising the bar for professionalism, ethics, and expertise. It has become a symbol of excellence and a key differentiator for wealth management professionals. With the growing complexity and sophistication of financial markets and products, clients have become more discerning in their choice of advisors. The CWM designation has become a trusted mark of competence, credibility, and commitment to ethical standards in the eyes of clients. Furthermore, the CWM designation has also had a significant influence on the development and evolution of wealth management as a whole. As more and more professionals seek out the certification, there is an increased emphasis on continuous learning, innovation, and delivering value-added services to clients. This has led to the development of advanced wealth management techniques, such as estate planning, tax management, and client relationship management, which are now integral components of the CWM certification.

Evolution of Wealth Management

The evolution of wealth management has been a dynamic and ongoing process, driven by changes in global economies, financial markets, and client expectations. Historically, wealth management was focused primarily on investment management and asset allocation. However, with the advent of the CWM designation and the increasing complexity of financial markets, the scope of wealth management has expanded to encompass a wider range of services. Today, wealth management is a holistic approach to managing the financial affairs of high net worth individuals and families. It goes beyond traditional investment management and incorporates various aspects of financial planning, tax management, and estate planning. Wealth management professionals with the CWM designation are equipped to provide comprehensive and integrated solutions to their clients, taking into consideration their unique financial goals, risk tolerance, and values.

An Uncommon Perspective

One of the key factors that sets the CWM designation apart from other certifications in the financial industry is its global perspective. The CWM certification is recognized in over 120 countries, providing a standardized and globally-relevant framework for wealth management professionals. This global perspective is particularly important in today's interconnected and fast-paced world, where clients often have assets and interests in multiple countries. Moreover, the CWM curriculum goes beyond technical knowledge and also emphasizes the importance of behavioral finance and client communication. This uncommon emphasis on the human element of wealth management sets CWM professionals apart from their peers, as they are trained to understand and address the emotional as well as financial aspects of managing wealth. In addition, the CWM certification also requires ongoing continuing education, ensuring that professionals stay up-to-date with the latest developments in the industry and are able to adapt to changing market conditions and client needs. This commitment to continuous improvement and learning is a key factor in the evolution of wealth management and sets CWM professionals apart as innovative and forward-thinking leaders in the field. In conclusion, the CWM designation has played a significant role in the evolution of wealth management, shaping the industry into a highly specialized and sophisticated field. Its impact can be seen in the increased professionalism and credibility of wealth management professionals, as well as the expanded scope of services offered. With its global perspective, emphasis on behavioral finance, and commitment to ongoing education, the CWM certification continues to be at the forefront of shaping the future of wealth management.

Chapter 3: The Importance of Estate Planning

Importance of Estate Planning

Estate planning may not be the most exciting aspect of wealth management, but it is certainly one of the most important. It is the process of organizing and planning for the distribution of one's assets after they pass away. Many people tend to shy away from this topic, either because they find it daunting or they simply do not want to think about their eventual passing. However, having a well-thought-out estate plan can provide peace of mind, protect loved ones, and ensure that your legacy continues on. One of the greatest advantages of estate planning is the ability to have control over what happens to your assets. Without a plan in place, the distribution of your assets will be left up to the laws of your state, which might not align with your wishes. With estate planning, you can specify who will receive what and when they will receive it. You can also include specific instructions for any unique or uncommon assets you may have, such as a beloved piece of art or a prized collection.

Basic Concepts

While estate planning may seem like a complex and intimidating process, at its core, it is quite simple. There are a few basic concepts that are important to understand when it comes to estate planning. First and foremost is the concept of probate. Probate is the legal process of validating a will and distributing assets after a person's passing. This process can be time-consuming, expensive, and open to the public. With proper estate planning, you can potentially avoid or minimize the probate process, saving your loved ones time, money, and privacy. Another important concept is that of guardianship. If you have minor children, it is crucial to have a plan in place for their care in the event of your passing. This can involve selecting a guardian and outlining their responsibilities and wishes for your children's upbringing. Without a designated guardian, the court will make this decision, which may not align with your wishes. Finally, another essential concept in estate planning is taxes. With proper planning, you can potentially minimize the amount of taxes that your estate will owe, leaving more for your loved ones. This can involve utilizing trusts, charitable giving, and other strategies.

Goals

When it comes to estate planning, it is crucial to have clear goals in mind. These goals will guide your decisions and help ensure that your estate plan aligns with your wishes. Some common estate planning goals include:

- Providing for loved ones: Perhaps one of the most common goals of estate planning is to ensure that loved ones are taken care of after one's passing. This can involve leaving assets to family members, providing for the financial needs of a spouse, or setting up a trust for children or grandchildren.

- Avoiding conflict: Without a well-written estate plan, there is a higher chance of family conflict arising after one's passing. Having a clear plan in place can help avoid any misunderstandings or disputes among family members.

- Philanthropy: Many people use estate planning as a way to leave a legacy through charitable giving. This can involve setting up a foundation, leaving assets to a specific charity, or creating a charitable trust.

- Minimizing taxes: As mentioned, estate planning can help reduce the amount of taxes that your estate will owe. With proper planning, you can potentially leave more for your loved ones and less for the government.

- Preservation of assets: Estate planning can also involve strategies for protecting assets from potential creditors or lawsuits. This can bring peace of mind and safeguard your hard-earned wealth. In conclusion, estate planning may not be the most exciting or glamorous aspect of wealth management, but it is a crucial one. It allows you to have control over what happens to your assets after you pass away and ensures that your loved ones are taken care of.

By understanding the basic concepts and setting clear goals, you can create a comprehensive estate plan that aligns with your wishes and provides peace of mind for both you and your loved ones.

Chapter 4: Types of Clients for Wealth Management

Wealth management is a specialized field that caters to individuals and families with significant financial assets. These individuals, known as High Net Worth Individuals (HNWIs), have unique needs and goals when it comes to managing their wealth. In this chapter, we will explore the different types of clients that a Chartered Wealth Manager (CWM) may encounter and the specific considerations that must be taken into account when providing wealth management services to them.

High Net Worth Individuals

HNWIs are individuals with a net worth of at least $1 million, excluding their primary residence. As of 2019, there are approximately 18.6 million HNWIs globally, with the majority residing in the United States, China, and Japan. These individuals have achieved a high level of success in their careers or businesses, and their assets may be derived from various sources such as inheritance, investments, and entrepreneurship. Managing the wealth of HNWIs requires a specialized skill set that goes beyond traditional financial planning. These individuals may have complex financial situations, including multiple sources of income, diverse investment portfolios, and potential tax implications. As a CWM, it is essential to have a deep understanding of the various strategies and solutions available to help HNWIs achieve their financial goals. One area that sets HNWIs apart from other clients is their appetite for risk. Due to their significant financial resources, they may be more willing to take on higher levels of risk in pursuit of higher returns. However, it is crucial to assess their risk tolerance and investment goals carefully. As we know, it is not wise to put all eggs in one basket, and diversification is key to mitigating risk in any investment portfolio.

Business Owners

Business owners often fall under the category of HNWIs, but their financial needs and goals may differ significantly from those of other high net worth individuals. These individuals have built their wealth through entrepreneurship and may have a more significant portion of their assets tied up in their business. As a result, they may require unique strategies for managing their wealth that take into account their business interests, such as succession planning and tax-efficient strategies for selling a business. Moreover, business owners may also face additional challenges when it comes to estate planning. In many cases, they have a strong desire to keep their business within the family, which can complicate the transfer of assets to their heirs. As a CWM, it is crucial to work closely with business owners to create a comprehensive plan that addresses their specific needs and goals and ensures the continuity of their business for future generations.

Family Offices

For ultra-high net worth individuals with a net worth of at least $30 million, the services of a CWM may not be enough. These individuals often turn to family offices, which are private wealth management firms that cater exclusively to the financial needs of a single family. Family offices provide a range of services, including investment management, estate planning, tax planning, and philanthropic planning. Managing the wealth of ultra-high net worth families can be a complex and challenging task that goes beyond traditional wealth management. It requires a deep understanding of the family's values, dynamics, and long-term goals. As a CWM, you may work closely with a family office to provide specialized expertise in areas such as investment management, risk management, and succession planning.

The Uncommon Things

While every client's financial situation is unique, there are some common considerations that must be taken into account when working with HNWIs, business owners, and families with ultra-high net worths. As a CWM, you must have a thorough understanding of the tax implications of different investment strategies, the complex rules and regulations surrounding estate planning, and the volatile nature of the financial markets. Moreover, you must also possess excellent communication skills to work effectively with different types of clients and various professionals, such as lawyers and accountants, to develop comprehensive wealth management plans. Moreover, it is crucial to recognize that wealth management is not just about accumulating wealth; it is also about preserving and transferring it to future generations. As a CWM, you must have a long-term perspective and help your clients make informed decisions that align with their values and goals. It requires staying up-to-date with the latest market changes, continuously learning and adapting to new strategies and solutions, and providing personalized and holistic advice to your clients.

In conclusion, managing the wealth of HNWIs, business owners, and ultra-high net worth families goes beyond traditional financial planning. It requires a specialized and comprehensive approach that considers their unique circumstances, goals, and values. As a CWM, it is your responsibility to provide tailored solutions and expert guidance to help your clients achieve their financial objectives and create a legacy that lasts for generations.

Chapter 5: Ethical Standards for CWM

Code of Conduct

Ethics and integrity are the cornerstones of the Chartered Wealth Manager (CWM) designation. As a CWM, you are committed to upholding the highest standards of professional conduct and ethical behavior in your interactions with clients, colleagues, and the financial community. But what exactly does this code of conduct entail? It is not just a list of rules or a set of guidelines to follow, but rather a mindset and a way of conducting oneself that goes beyond the surface level. It is about values, principles, and a strong moral compass that guides you in all aspects of your professional and personal life. One of the key elements of the CWM code of conduct is honesty and transparency. This means being open and truthful with your clients, disclosing any potential conflicts of interest, and always acting in their best interests. It also means being accountable for your actions and taking responsibility for any mistakes or errors. As a CWM, you are also expected to maintain confidentiality with your clients' personal and financial information. This not only builds trust with your clients but also demonstrates your professionalism and respect for their privacy. It is important to remember that you have been entrusted with sensitive information and it is your duty to protect it at all times. Another important aspect of the CWM code of conduct is fairness and non-discrimination. This means treating all clients and colleagues with equal respect and not discriminating based on factors such as race, gender, religion, or sexual orientation. It also means being mindful of any biases or prejudices you may have and actively working to overcome them.

Fiduciary Duty

As a CWM, you have a fiduciary duty to your clients, which is the highest legal standard of care. This means that you are legally obligated to act in good faith and in the best interests of your clients, putting their needs above your own. This duty extends not only to your actions but also to your recommendations and advice. What does this mean in practical terms? It means always providing objective and unbiased advice, even if it does not personally benefit you. It means thoroughly understanding your clients' financial goals and risk tolerance before making any investment recommendations. And it means monitoring and reassessing their portfolios regularly to ensure they remain in line with their objectives. But fiduciary duty goes beyond just providing financial advice. It also includes being a trusted advisor and advocate for your clients. This may involve helping them make sound financial decisions, educating them on complex financial concepts, and helping them stay on track towards their goals.

Professionalism

Being a CWM means more than just having a set of technical skills and knowledge. It also requires a high level of professionalism and conduct. This includes maintaining a professional appearance, being punctual and responsive, and communicating effectively with clients and colleagues. But professionalism is more than just appearances and behavior. It also encompasses a strong work ethic and commitment to continuous learning and development. As a CWM, you are expected to stay up-to-date on industry trends and advancements, continuously improve your skills, and adhere to the highest standards of excellence in your work. In addition, CWM professionals are expected to uphold the reputation and integrity of the designation. This means being honest and ethical in all your dealings and avoiding any actions that could bring discredit to yourself or the CWM community. In conclusion, the code of conduct, fiduciary duty, and professionalism of the CWM designation go hand in hand to create a strong foundation for ethical behavior and high-quality service. As a CWM, you are not only responsible for managing your clients' wealth but also for upholding the values and principles of the designation. Embrace these responsibilities with pride and dedication, and you will not only be a successful CWM but also a valuable member of the financial community.

Chapter 6: Asset Allocation and Portfolio Management

Allocation Strategies

When it comes to managing investments, one of the most critical decisions is determining the proper asset allocation. This involves deciding how much to invest in different asset classes, such as stocks, bonds, and cash equivalents. While this decision may seem straightforward, there are many factors to consider. Traditional allocation strategies often involve diversifying assets based on their risk and return profiles. For example, younger individuals with a longer investment horizon may have a higher allocation to stocks, while older individuals may have a higher allocation to bonds or cash equivalents. However, with the rise of alternative investments and the ever-changing market landscape, a one-size-fits-all approach may not be the most effective. Instead, a more customized approach may be necessary, taking into account an individual's specific goals, risk tolerance, and investment horizon. This may involve using multiple allocation strategies, such as tactical allocation or dynamic asset allocation, to adjust the portfolio based on the current market conditions.

Diversification

One of the most common phrases in investing is "Don't put all your eggs in one basket." This idea applies to portfolio management as well. Diversification is the practice of spreading investments across different asset classes, industries, and geographies to reduce risk and increase potential returns. However, diversification goes beyond just spreading investments across different asset classes. It also involves looking at the underlying holdings within each asset class. For example, within the stock market, there are large-cap, mid-cap, and small-cap companies, as well as international and emerging market companies. By diversifying within each asset class, investors can further reduce risk and potentially improve overall portfolio performance. In addition to asset class and size diversification, investors should also consider diversifying across investment styles. This includes growth, value, and blend investment styles, which may perform differently in various market environments. Incorporating alternative investments, such as real estate, private equity, and commodities, can also add another layer of diversification to a portfolio.

Risk Management

No investment strategy is without risk, and as the saying goes, "The higher the risk, the higher the potential reward." While investors may be comfortable with some level of risk, it is essential to manage it effectively. One way to manage risk is through ongoing portfolio monitoring and rebalancing. Regularly assessing portfolio performance and making adjustments to risk levels can help ensure the portfolio aligns with the investor's goals and risk tolerance. Investors can also utilize tools such as stop-loss orders, which can help limit losses during market downturns. Diversification and asset allocation can also play a role in risk management, spreading risk across different investments and limiting exposure to any one asset. It is also important to consider taxes when managing risk. Tax-loss harvesting, where investors sell losing investments to offset gains from other investments, can help manage taxes and potentially increase overall portfolio returns. Moreover, having a solid understanding of behavioral finance can also aid in managing risk. Emotions can often drive investment decisions, leading to poor results. By educating clients on the importance of staying disciplined and avoiding emotional decision-making, advisors can help manage risk and set clients on a path towards long-term success.

Uncommon Approaches

While traditional allocation strategies and diversification techniques are commonly used, there are also alternative approaches that investors and advisors can consider. One such approach is goal-based investing. This involves aligning investment decisions with specific financial goals. Rather than focusing solely on maximizing returns, investors and advisors can focus on achieving specific outcomes, such as retirement income or funding a child's education. Another uncommon approach is utilizing tactical asset allocation. This strategy involves making short-term adjustments to the portfolio based on changing market conditions and economic data. By actively monitoring and adjusting the portfolio, investors can potentially improve returns and manage risk. Furthermore, incorporating environmental, social, and governance (ESG) factors into the investment process can add another layer of diversification. ESG investing considers not only financial performance but also environmental and social impact and corporate governance practices. This can allow investors and advisors to align their investments with their values and potentially reduce risk. In conclusion, asset allocation and portfolio management are crucial components of successful wealth management. By understanding and utilizing various allocation strategies, diversification techniques, and risk management tools, investors and advisors can help clients reach their financial goals while managing risk. And by considering uncommon approaches, such as goal-based investing and ESG investing, advisors can provide a more personalized and comprehensive approach to portfolio management.

Chapter 7: Estate Planning Process

Estate planning is a crucial component of wealth management, as it ensures that your assets and legacy are protected and transferred according to your wishes. This process involves gathering important information, analyzing goals and objectives, and creating a comprehensive plan. However, there is more to estate planning than just ensuring a smooth transfer of assets. It also involves addressing potential challenges and considering unique scenarios that may arise. In this chapter, we will dive deeper into the estate planning process and discuss uncommon factors that should be addressed to create a solid plan.

Gathering Information

The first step in the estate planning process is gathering all of the necessary information. This includes documents such as wills, trusts, insurance policies, financial statements, and investments. It is important to review these documents regularly to ensure they are up-to-date and accurately reflect your current wishes. Additionally, it is important to think beyond just financial assets. Consider any digital assets, such as online accounts and social media profiles, and how you want them to be handled after your passing. Another crucial aspect of gathering information is understanding the unique dynamics of your family and relationships. This may include planning for special needs family members, business partners, and blended families. These factors may complicate the distribution of assets and should be addressed in your plan.

Analyzing Goals and Objectives

Once you have gathered all of the necessary information, the next step is to analyze your goals and objectives for your estate. This involves considering your values, beliefs, and desires for your assets and legacy. It may also involve discussions with family members to ensure everyone is on the same page. In addition to traditional goals of wealth preservation and transfer, it is also important to consider any philanthropic goals or desires to leave a lasting impact through charitable giving. This may involve setting up a charitable trust or foundation to support causes that are important to you.

Creating a Plan

Based on the information gathered and goals established, the final step is to create a comprehensive estate plan. This plan should document how your assets will be distributed and managed after your passing, address any tax and legal considerations, and provide instructions for end-of-life healthcare wishes. In addition to traditional aspects of estate planning, there are some uncommon factors that should also be addressed. For example, many people may not consider what would happen if they were to become incapacitated or unable to make decisions for themselves. In this case, a power of attorney and advanced healthcare directive should be included in the plan to designate someone to make decisions on your behalf. Another often overlooked aspect is addressing digital assets. With the rise of technology and importance of online accounts, it is crucial to have a plan for how these assets will be handled after your passing. Some online platforms have specific policies in place for how to address a deceased person's account, so it is important to research and include these in your plan. Lastly, it is important to review and update your estate plan regularly to ensure it reflects any changes in your life or goals. This may include updates to beneficiary designations, changes in tax laws, or births and deaths in the family. In conclusion, the estate planning process is a crucial aspect of wealth management that involves gathering information, analyzing goals and objectives, and creating a comprehensive plan. However, it is important to also consider uncommon factors and address potential challenges that may arise to ensure your legacy is protected and your wishes are carried out. By working with a qualified wealth manager and regularly reviewing and updating your plan, you can have peace of mind in knowing that your assets and legacy are in good hands.

Chapter 8: Tax Planning and Management

When it comes to wealth management, it's not just about growing and preserving your assets, but also about minimizing tax liability. Taxes can greatly impact your overall wealth and financial goals, which is why having a thorough understanding of tax planning and management strategies is crucial for any Chartered Wealth Manager (CWM).

Types of Taxes

Many people think of income tax as the only type of tax they have to worry about. However, there are various types of taxes that can affect your finances. These include income tax, capital gains tax, estate tax, gift tax, and property tax. Each type of tax has its own rules and regulations, making tax planning an intricate and complex process.

Strategies for Minimizing Tax Liability

Fortunately, there are several strategies that can help minimize your tax liability and optimize your overall wealth. One common strategy is to take advantage of tax-deferred investment vehicles, such as retirement accounts and annuities. By deferring taxes on your investments, you have the opportunity to grow your money tax-free until you withdraw them during retirement. Another approach is to diversify your investments. By having a mix of taxable and tax-free investments, you can balance out the tax burden and potentially lower your overall tax rate. Additionally, utilizing tax-loss harvesting can help offset gains in your portfolio and reduce your tax liability.

Tax Efficient Investing

When it comes to investing, it's important to not only focus on the returns, but also the tax implications. Tax-efficient investing involves structuring your investments in a way that minimizes the amount of taxes you owe. This can include investing in tax-free municipal bonds or using tax-efficient index funds. Charitable giving is also a tax-efficient way to manage your wealth. By donating to qualified charities, you can receive a tax deduction that can lower your overall tax bill. Additionally, setting up a donor-advised fund can provide even greater tax benefits and flexibility in your charitable giving.

Uncommon Tax Strategies

As a CWM, it's important to think outside the box when it comes to tax planning and management. One uncommon strategy is gifting appreciated assets to family members. By doing so, you can pass on the assets to your loved ones without them having to pay capital gains tax on the appreciated value. You can also use a trust to protect your assets and minimize estate and gift taxes. Another uncommon approach is to take advantage of retirement account conversions. By converting traditional IRA funds to a Roth IRA, you can potentially lower your future tax burden and have tax-free distributions during retirement. However, this strategy requires careful planning and consideration of your individual tax situation.

The Importance of Staying Up-to-Date

Tax laws and regulations are constantly changing, which is why it's crucial for CWMs to continuously educate themselves and stay up-to-date on tax planning strategies. This not only benefits your clients, but also your own financial situation. Not staying on top of changes and updates can result in missed opportunities for tax savings or even unexpected tax liabilities. In addition to staying knowledgeable, it's important to communicate and collaborate with other tax professionals, such as accountants and tax attorneys. Working together with a team of experts can ensure that your clients' tax planning and management needs are being met in the most efficient and effective way.

The Bottom Line

Tax planning and management are crucial aspects of wealth management that must not be overlooked. By understanding the various types of taxes and implementing strategic approaches, CWMs can help their clients minimize their tax liability and optimize their overall wealth. Continuous education and collaboration with other professionals are key to success in this ever-changing landscape of tax laws and regulations. As a CWM, it's important to stay proactive and always be on the lookout for new and innovative tax planning strategies.

Chapter 9: Client Relationship Management

Building Trust

Building trust is crucial in any professional relationship, but it is of utmost importance in wealth management. As a Chartered Wealth Manager, your clients are trusting you with their financial future and it is essential to establish a strong foundation of trust in order to achieve success in your role. One way to build trust is to provide your clients with transparency. Be open and honest about your expertise, services, and fees. This level of transparency can help ease any apprehension or doubts your clients may have. In addition, be sure to practice what you preach. Show your clients that you follow the same principles and strategies you recommend to them, as this will give them confidence in your abilities. Another key aspect of building trust is being a good listener. While you may have years of experience and knowledge, it is important to listen to your clients' needs, goals, and concerns. This shows that you not only care about their financial well-being but also that you value their input. By truly understanding your clients' needs, you can tailor your services and develop a personalized wealth management plan for each individual.

Communication Strategies

Effective communication is vital in any relationship, and this holds true in wealth management as well. As a CWM, you must be an expert in communicating financial information to your clients in a clear and concise manner. This not only helps in building trust but also ensures that your clients understand and are comfortable with the strategies being implemented. One way to improve your communication with clients is through active listening. This involves giving your full attention to the client, understanding their concerns, and responding thoughtfully. By actively listening, you can gather valuable information that will help you tailor your services to best meet their needs. Another valuable communication strategy is providing regular updates and reports to your clients. This shows that you are engaged and involved in managing their wealth and reassures them that their financial goals are being addressed. These reports can also serve as a platform for you to showcase your expertise and educate your clients on various financial topics.

Handling Difficult Situations

As a wealth manager, you may encounter difficult situations that require quick and effective decision-making. These could be market downturns, unexpected changes in a client's personal or financial situation, or other external factors that can affect their wealth. It is important to have a plan in place to handle such situations with professionalism and ease. One approach to handling difficult situations is to remain calm and composed. This not only demonstrates your expertise but also helps to reassure clients that their financial well-being is a top priority for you. Additionally, provide your clients with all the necessary information and options, so they can make informed decisions. It is also important to be proactive in identifying potential issues and addressing them before they become bigger problems. Furthermore, it is essential to maintain open and honest communication during difficult times. This will help in managing expectations and preventing any misunderstandings or mistrust between you and your clients. In conclusion, as a Chartered Wealth Manager, your client relationships are crucial to your success. By building trust, effectively communicating, and handling difficult situations with professionalism, you can establish long-lasting relationships with your clients. Remember, it is not just about managing their wealth, but also about providing them with a sense of security and peace of mind for their financial future.

Chapter 10: Investment Vehicles

Stocks

When discussing investments, stocks often come to mind as they have been a popular choice for decades. Stocks, or equities, represent ownership in a company and can potentially provide high returns over time. However, investing in stocks also comes with a higher level of risk. It is important for CWMs to thoroughly research and analyze a company before investing in their stocks. Uncommon fact: Did you know that there are different types of stocks? Common stocks, which are the most well-known, give shareholders voting rights and potential dividends. On the other hand, preferred stocks do not provide voting rights but pay out fixed dividends.

Bonds

Bonds are considered a more conservative investment compared to stocks. They are essentially loans made to a government or company, with the promise of receiving back the amount borrowed plus interest. Bonds tend to have a lower risk but also lower returns compared to stocks. Uncommon fact: Did you know that bonds can also be risky? Bond issuers can default on their payments, leading to potential losses for investors. It is important for CWMs to assess the creditworthiness of the issuer before investing in bonds.

Mutual Funds

Mutual funds are pools of money collected from investors and managed by a professional fund manager. They buy a variety of securities, such as stocks, bonds, and other assets, giving investors access to a diversified portfolio. This reduces risks and can potentially yield higher returns compared to investing in individual assets. Uncommon fact: Did you know that there are actively and passively managed mutual funds? Actively managed funds are actively monitored and adjusted by a fund manager, while passively managed funds simply track an index, such as the S&P 500. CWMs can help clients choose the right type of mutual fund depending on their risk tolerance and investment goals.

Real Estate

Real estate is another popular investment choice, whether through owning physical property or investing in real estate investment trusts (REITs). Real estate can provide consistent rental income and long-term appreciation, but it also comes with associated costs and the risk of market fluctuations. Uncommon fact: Did you know that there are different types of real estate investments? Residential properties are the most common, but there are also commercial, industrial, and even agricultural properties that can be invested in. CWMs can help clients diversify their real estate portfolio based on their financial goals.

Alternative Investments

Alternative investments cover a wide range of assets, from private equity and hedge funds to collectibles like art and wine. These investments are typically not as accessible to the general public and can carry higher risk, but they also offer the potential for high returns. Uncommon fact: Did you know that wine has been consistently outperforming art as an investment? According to data from the Wall Street Journal, fine wine has proven to be a more reliable and profitable alternative investment compared to art. CWMs can explore unique and unexpected opportunities for their clients within the world of alternative investments.

Investing with a CWM

As a CWM, it is important to understand the different types of investment vehicles and how they can benefit clients. Each client will have their own unique financial goals and risk tolerance levels, and it is the CWM's responsibility to create a tailored investment plan that aligns with these factors. Through thorough research and analysis, CWMs can help clients build a diversified portfolio that can weather market fluctuations and potentially yield higher returns. Additionally, constant monitoring and assessments of the portfolio can help CWMs make changes and adjustments as needed to ensure their clients' investments align with their financial goals. In this chapter, we have discussed some of the most common investment vehicles, as well as some lesser-known facts about them. As a CWM, it is crucial to stay informed and educated on the constantly evolving world of investments in order to provide the best guidance and support to clients. By utilizing a variety of investment vehicles and techniques, CWMs can help clients reach their long-term financial goals and achieve financial success.

Chapter 11: Estate and Trust Law

Legal Framework

When it comes to estate and trust law, it's important to understand the legal framework in which these concepts operate. This includes understanding the different laws and regulations that govern estate planning and trust administration, as well as any relevant tax laws. While estate and trust laws may differ from country to country, many overarching principles remain the same, such as the protection of assets and the distribution of wealth. However, it's also important to note that estate and trust laws are continuously evolving, so it's crucial for Chartered Wealth Managers (CWM) to stay up to date on any changes or updates that may affect their clients' estate plans or trust structures. This requires a deep understanding of legal principles and the ability to navigate through complex laws and regulations.

Types of Trusts

There are several types of trusts that Chartered Wealth Managers may encounter when working with their clients. These include revocable trusts, irrevocable trusts, and living trusts. Each type has specific features and benefits, and it's important for CWMs to understand the intricacies of each one in order to provide the best advice for their clients. Revocable trusts allow the grantor (the person who creates the trust) to make changes, withdraw assets, or terminate the trust at any time. This type of trust is often used for asset protection and financial privacy. On the other hand, irrevocable trusts cannot be changed or terminated without the permission of the trust beneficiaries. This type of trust is often used for estate tax planning and asset protection. Living trusts, also known as inter vivos trusts, are created during the lifetime of the grantor and can be revocable or irrevocable. They can provide many benefits, such as avoiding probate and managing assets in the event of incapacity. There are also more specialized trusts that may be used for specific purposes, such as bypass trusts for married couples, special needs trusts for individuals with disabilities, and pet trusts for the care of beloved animals. With so many options available, it's crucial for CWMs to have a deep understanding of trust laws and their various uses.

Administration and Distribution

Once a trust has been created, it's important for the CWM to understand the proper administration and distribution procedures. This may include managing investments, complying with tax laws, and ensuring proper distribution of assets to beneficiaries according to the trust's terms. Trust administration can be a complex and time-consuming process, but with the help of a CWM, clients can have peace of mind knowing that their assets are being managed and distributed in accordance with their wishes. Additionally, it's important for CWMs to provide their clients with ongoing support and assistance in reviewing and updating their trust documents as needed. It's also worth mentioning that there may be unique challenges or uncommon situations that arise in trust administration and distribution, which is why it's important for CWMs to have a deep understanding of the legal framework and trust laws in order to provide the best guidance and solutions for their clients. In conclusion, estate and trust law is a critical aspect of wealth management, and it requires a sophisticated and educated approach. By understanding the legal framework, types of trusts, and administration and distribution processes, CWMs can provide their clients with comprehensive and effective estate planning and trust management services. However, it's also important for CWMs to constantly stay informed and adapt to any changes in laws and regulations, in order to provide the best possible advice and solutions for their clients.

Chapter 12: Financial Planning for Retirement

Retirement is a time of great transition, where one leaves the workforce and begins a new chapter in life. It is a stage that many people dream of and work towards throughout their working years. So, it is important for individuals to have a clear understanding of their retirement goals and how to achieve them. As a Chartered Wealth Manager (CWM), it is essential to assist clients in planning for their retirement and addressing any concerns they may have. In this chapter, we will discuss various aspects of financial planning for retirement, including social security, annuities, and long-term care insurance.

Retirement Goals

The first step in planning for retirement is to understand what your goals are. These can vary from person to person, but some common goals include traveling, pursuing hobbies, spending time with family, and maintaining a comfortable standard of living. It is crucial to have a clear vision of what you want your retirement to look like, as it will serve as a guide for your financial planning. It is also important to consider the duration of your retirement. With advancements and improvements in healthcare, people are living longer and healthier lives. It means that your retirement could potentially last for 20-30 years, and you need to plan accordingly to ensure your financial stability during that time. Many individuals also have concerns about how much money they will need for retirement. It is a complex question with no one-size-fits-all answer. It is crucial to take into account factors such as your current lifestyle and expenses, inflation rates, and potential healthcare costs in retirement. As a CWM, it is important to work closely with your clients to understand their specific retirement goals and create a personalized financial plan that will help them achieve those goals.

Social Security

One of the key components of retirement planning is understanding social security benefits. Social Security is a federal program that provides a source of income for retirees and individuals with disabilities. It is funded through payroll taxes and is a significant source of retirement income for many Americans. To qualify for Social Security benefits, one must have worked and paid Social Security taxes for a certain number of years. The amount of benefits received depends on factors such as earnings history, the age at which the benefits are claimed, and the number of years worked. An important consideration for retirees is the age at which they choose to start receiving Social Security benefits. While individuals can claim benefits as early as 62 years old, it is advisable to wait until full retirement age, which is typically 66-67 years, to receive the full amount. Delaying benefits can also result in higher monthly payments. As a CWM, it is essential to educate clients on how Social Security works and how it fits into their overall retirement plan. It is also crucial to factor in potential changes or adjustments to the program in the future.

Annuities

Annuities are a type of financial product often used for retirement planning. They work similarly to a personal pension plan, where individuals make contributions over a period of time, and the funds are invested. In return, the annuity provides a steady stream of income during retirement. There are various types of annuities, including fixed, variable, and indexed annuities. Each type offers different features and benefits, such as a guaranteed income stream, potential for growth, and tax-deferred growth. Annuities can be a valuable tool for retirement planning, but they also come with various fees and complexities. As a CWM, it is important to thoroughly educate clients on the features and potential drawbacks of annuities, and determine if and how they fit into their retirement plan.

Long-term Care Insurance

Long-term care insurance is an insurance policy that covers the costs of long-term care, such as home or nursing care, for individuals who are unable to care for themselves. As people are living longer, the likelihood of needing long-term care in retirement is increasing. Long-term care insurance can help protect retirement savings from being depleted due to unexpected healthcare costs. Similar to other forms of insurance, long-term care insurance requires individuals to pay premiums for coverage. The cost of the premiums depends on factors such as age, health status, and the level of coverage. It is important for individuals to consider the potential need for long-term care and discuss with their CWM if long-term care insurance is a viable option for them.

Uncommon Considerations

When planning for retirement, it is vital to consider any uncommon or unexpected factors that may impact your financial stability. For example, many people do not account for potential health issues or care for aging family members in their retirement plan. It is crucial to have a contingency plan in place in case of these situations. As a CWM, it is important to discuss and address any uncommon considerations with clients to ensure they have a well-rounded retirement plan.

Conclusion

Retirement planning is a complex and multi-faceted process. As a CWM, it is crucial to work closely with clients to understand their retirement goals and create a personalized plan that addresses all aspects, including social security, annuities, and long-term care insurance. By taking a holistic approach and considering both common and uncommon factors, we can help our clients achieve a comfortable and financially stable retirement. Let's work together to make their retirement dreams a reality.

Chapter 13: Advanced Retirement Strategies

As we approach retirement, many of us start to assess our financial situation and evaluate our retirement goals. However, there are more than just financial factors to consider when planning for retirement. It is important to also consider the impact of taxes, charitable giving, and succession planning on your retirement strategy. In this chapter, we will explore advanced retirement strategies that take into account these additional factors.

Tax Planning

When planning for retirement, it is essential to consider the role of taxes. Many people assume that their taxes will decrease in retirement, but this is not always the case. In fact, taxes can have a significant impact on your retirement income and overall financial plan. One strategy to minimize taxes during retirement is to utilize tax-deferred retirement accounts such as a 401(k) or traditional IRA. By contributing to these accounts while working, you can decrease your taxable income and potentially lower your tax bill. Additionally, withdrawals from these accounts are taxed at retirement, when your income may be lower than during your working years. It is also important to consider the impact of required minimum distributions (RMDs) on your taxes during retirement. Once you reach age 70 ½, you are required to withdraw a certain percentage from your traditional IRA and pay taxes on the distribution. However, by strategically planning your withdrawals, you may be able to minimize your tax liability. Another factor to consider is the tax implications of Social Security benefits. If you have additional sources of income during retirement, your Social Security benefits may become taxable. Working with a tax professional can help you understand how to minimize the tax impact of your Social Security benefits.

Charitable Giving

Many individuals and families choose to incorporate charitable giving into their retirement strategies. Not only does giving back to the community provide a sense of purpose and fulfillment during retirement, but it can also have significant tax benefits. One strategy to consider is gifting appreciated assets to charity. By donating stocks or other assets that have increased in value, you may be able to avoid paying capital gains tax on the appreciation. Additionally, charitable donations can also lower your income tax liability. There are also more complex strategies for charitable giving, such as setting up a charitable remainder trust or a donor-advised fund. These options allow you to donate assets to a charitable organization while also receiving a tax benefit and potentially generating income for yourself or your heirs.

Succession Planning

While retirement may seem far off, it is important to consider the long-term impact of your financial decisions on your family and loved ones. Succession planning is the process of determining how assets will be transferred to the next generation and ensuring that your wishes are carried out. One aspect of succession planning is choosing the right beneficiaries for your retirement accounts and insurance policies. By designating beneficiaries, you can ensure that your assets are distributed according to your wishes, and potentially minimize taxes for your heirs. Another important consideration is estate planning. Working with an estate planning attorney and financial advisor can help you create a plan for the transfer of your assets that minimizes estate taxes and ensures that your loved ones are taken care of. In addition to these financial considerations, succession planning also involves creating a plan for your business if you are a business owner. This may include grooming a successor or developing a plan for the sale or transfer of your business to ensure its continued success. As you can see, advanced retirement strategies go beyond just saving and investing for retirement. By considering the impact of taxes, charitable giving, and succession planning on your retirement plan, you can create a more comprehensive and strategic approach to achieve your retirement goals.

In conclusion, planning for retirement is a multi-faceted endeavor that requires careful consideration of many factors. By incorporating advanced strategies related to taxes, charitable giving, and succession planning, you can optimize your retirement plan and leave a lasting legacy for your loved ones. Working with a skilled financial advisor who specializes in retirement planning can help you navigate these complex topics and create a personalized retirement strategy that aligns with your goals and values. Remember, the earlier you start planning, the better off you will be in the long run. So take control of your retirement plan today and enjoy a financially secure and fulfilling retirement.

Chapter 14: Understanding Investor Behavior - Emotion-based Decision Making and Overcoming Biases

Investing is not just about numbers and charts, it also involves human emotions and behavior. As a Chartered Wealth Manager, it is essential to understand the psychology behind investor decision making and the impact it can have on their portfolios. In this chapter, we will delve into the world of investor behavior, how emotions drive decision making, and ways to overcome biases to make better investment choices.

Understanding Investor Behavior

Investor behavior refers to how investors react and make decisions about their investments. It is a crucial aspect of wealth management as it can greatly influence portfolio performance. Many factors contribute to investor behavior, such as risk tolerance, investment goals, and market conditions. As CWMs, we must understand these different elements and how they can affect clients' investment decisions. Research has shown that investors tend to be more risk-averse when it comes to losses than gains. This phenomenon is known as "loss aversion." It means that investors are more distressed by potential losses than they are excited by potential gains. Understanding this can help us tailor our investment strategies to align with clients' risk tolerance and help them avoid making rash decisions based on fear of loss.

Emotion-based Decision Making

Emotions play a significant role in investor behavior. When faced with a potential gain or loss, emotions can cloud investors' rational thinking and cause them to make impulsive decisions. For example, when a stock they own is performing well, investors may feel an emotional high and be more likely to hold on to it, even if it is overvalued. On the other hand, when a stock is declining, investors may panic and sell, causing them to miss out on potential gains. As CWMs, we must help our clients understand the impact of emotions on their investment decisions. We can do this by educating them about the importance of staying rational and not letting emotions drive their choices. By teaching clients how to detach themselves from their investments and view them objectively, we can help them make more sound and logical investment decisions.

Overcoming Biases

Biases are ingrained in human psychology, and they can significantly affect investment decisions. One common bias among investors is "anchoring," where they fixate on a specific price or number and refuse to let it go. This can cause them to hold on to an underperforming investment, hoping that it will bounce back to the initial price they paid. Another bias is "confirmation bias," where investors only seek information that confirms their beliefs and ignore evidence that contradicts them. As CWMs, it is our responsibility to help our clients identify and overcome biases that can hold them back from achieving their investment goals. By encouraging them to diversify their portfolios, focus on long-term goals, and not let past performance dictate future investments, we can help them overcome these biases and make more informed decisions. Understanding investor behavior and overcoming biases is crucial to successful wealth management. As CWMs, we must continuously educate ourselves on the latest research and trends in investor behavior to better serve our clients. By understanding how emotions and biases can impact investment decisions and helping our clients overcome them, we can build stronger, more resilient portfolios for our clients.

Uncommon Considerations

While most investors are familiar with common biases such as "loss aversion" and "confirmation bias," there are other, less talked about factors that can also affect investor behavior. One such factor is overconfidence. Many investors believe they have a good knowledge of the market and can pick winning investments, leading to overtrading and poor returns. Another uncommon consideration is the "house money effect," where investors are more likely to take risks with their gains than their original investment. This can lead to over-exposure in high-risk investments and potentially result in significant losses. As CWMs, we must educate our clients about these uncommon factors to help them make more informed decisions. In conclusion, as CWMs, we must understand the psychology behind investor behavior and the impact it can have on their portfolios. By recognizing the role of emotions, helping clients overcome biases, and addressing uncommon considerations, we can guide them towards making more rational and informed investment decisions. This is the key to achieving long-term financial success for our clients.

Chapter 15: Advanced Retirement Strategies

Retirement is a major milestone in one's life, and careful planning is essential to ensure a comfortable and enjoyable post-work life. As a Chartered Wealth Manager (CWM), it is your responsibility to help your clients navigate through this transition with ease and confidence. In this chapter, we will discuss some advanced retirement strategies that go beyond the traditional approaches and take a more comprehensive and holistic approach to retirement planning. So, let's dive in and explore these unconventional but effective strategies.

Strategies for Inheritance

Inheritance is often a sensitive and emotional topic, but it is also an essential aspect of retirement planning.

As a CWM, you must consider your client's family dynamics and the legacy they want to leave behind when crafting a retirement plan. One way to address this is through strategic inheritance planning. This involves considering factors like taxes, distribution of assets, and family relationships while deciding on the best way to transfer wealth to the next generation. For example, setting up a trust can help minimize taxes and protect assets from potential creditors. It also allows your client to have control over how their wealth is distributed after their passing. Another strategy is gifting assets during their lifetime, which can help reduce the tax burden on their estate. However, this approach requires careful consideration and should be done in consultation with a tax specialist to ensure it aligns with your client's overall financial goals.

Family Governance

As your clients near retirement, they start thinking about the legacy they want to leave behind for their loved ones. However, passing down wealth to the next generation can sometimes create conflicts and disagreements. That's where family governance comes in. It involves establishing guidelines and processes for the management of family wealth and decision-making around the transfer of assets. Encouraging open and honest communication among family members is a crucial aspect of family governance. This helps to set expectations and avoid misunderstandings and conflicts. It also allows family members to be involved in important financial decisions, which can help prepare them for the responsibilities that come with inheriting wealth. As a CWM, you can work alongside your clients to facilitate this dialogue and create a solid foundation for a successful and sustainable family legacy.

Philanthropy

Retirement not only marks the end of a career but also the beginning of a new phase in your client's life. As your clients shift from accumulating wealth to enjoying it, many of them become interested in giving back to society. Philanthropy can bring a sense of fulfillment and purpose to their retirement years. Therefore, as a CWM, it is essential to discuss philanthropic goals with your clients and incorporate them into their retirement plan. Philanthropy also has tax benefits, making it a powerful tool for advanced retirement planning. By making charitable contributions, your clients can reduce their taxable income and potentially lower their tax bill. Moreover, getting involved in philanthropic activities can bring new social connections and opportunities for your clients to stay engaged and active during retirement.

Uncommon Approaches to Advance Retirement Strategies

As a CWM, you are always thinking ahead and finding ways to help your clients achieve their financial goals. Here are a few less conventional strategies that may be beneficial in advanced retirement planning:

1. Timing Social Security Benefits: Encourage your clients to delay claiming their Social Security benefits until they reach their full retirement age or even later. This can increase their monthly benefit amount by up to 8% per year, ultimately resulting in higher income during retirement.

2. Leveraging Home Equity: If your clients own a home, they can use it to supplement income during retirement. They can downsize, rent out a portion of their property, or utilize reverse mortgages to access the equity in their home without having to sell it.

3. Long-Term Care Planning: Many retirees overlook the cost of long-term care, which can significantly impact their retirement savings. By including long-term care insurance in their retirement plan, your clients can have peace of mind knowing they are financially prepared for any potential health care needs.

Conclusion

Retirement planning goes beyond crunching numbers and creating a diversified investment portfolio. It requires a deeper understanding of your client's unique situation and goals. As a CWM, it is your job to guide your clients through the complexities of retirement planning and help them make informed decisions that align with their values and long-term objectives. By incorporating advanced strategies like strategic inheritance planning, family governance, and philanthropy, you can create a comprehensive retirement plan that not only secures your client's financial future but also leaves a lasting legacy for generations to come. In this chapter, we have explored some advanced retirement strategies that can help your clients make the most out of their retirement years. By thinking outside the box and considering factors like heir inheritance, family governance, and philanthropy, you can provide your clients with a holistic approach to retirement planning. So, as a CWM, keep these strategies in mind when working with clients on their retirement plan, and create a brighter future for them and their loved ones.

Chapter 16: Advanced Investment Strategies: Types, Uses, and Risks of Derivatives

Derivatives may sound like a complicated term, but in reality, they are just financial instruments that derive their value from an underlying asset. These assets could be stocks, bonds, commodities, or even currencies. In recent years, derivatives have gained a bad reputation due to their role in the financial crisis of 2008. However, these instruments are not inherently evil or risky. In fact, when used correctly, they can be powerful tools for managing risks and enhancing portfolio performance. In this chapter, we will delve into the world of derivatives and explore their types, uses in portfolio management, and how to manage risks associated with them.

Types of Derivatives

There are various types of derivatives, but the most common ones include options, futures, forwards, and swaps. Options give the holder the right, but not the obligation, to buy or sell an underlying asset at a predetermined price and date in the future. Futures, on the other hand, are contracts that require the parties involved to buy or sell an asset at a specific price on a specific date. Forwards are similar to futures, but they are not standardized contracts and are often used for over-the-counter transactions. Lastly, swaps are agreements between two parties to exchange cash flows according to specific terms. Each of these derivatives has its unique features and uses, making them suitable for different investment strategies.

Uses in Portfolio Management

Derivatives are often used as a risk management tool in portfolio management. For instance, buying put options can protect a stock portfolio from market downturns. In this scenario, the put option acts as an insurance policy, and if the stock price falls below a certain level, the option can be exercised, and the loss will be offset. Similarly, using futures contracts can hedge against changes in interest rates or currency fluctuations, reducing the portfolio's overall risk. Derivatives can also be used to enhance returns and generate income. For example, writing covered call options on stocks can generate an additional source of income for the portfolio.

Managing Risks

Like any other investment, derivatives come with their share of risks. The most significant danger is the potential for leverage. Derivatives are inherently leveraged instruments, meaning that a small movement in the underlying asset can result in a substantial gain or loss. It is vital to understand the risks associated with each type of derivative and their potential impact on the portfolio. Risk management techniques, such as position sizing and proper hedging, should be employed to mitigate the risks associated with derivatives effectively. It is also crucial to have a thorough understanding of the contracts and their terms before engaging in any derivative transaction. It is worth noting that derivatives are often used by institutional investors and sophisticated individual investors due to their complex nature. However, with proper education and guidance, retail investors can also incorporate derivatives into their portfolios. It is essential to consult with a qualified professional before making any investment decisions involving derivatives.

Uncommon Uses of Derivatives

While derivatives are commonly associated with risk management and hedging strategies, they have some unconventional uses as well. For instance, weather derivatives allow companies to hedge against losses due to adverse weather conditions. These contracts are particularly useful for businesses in industries such as agriculture, energy, and tourism. There are also emission derivatives, which are used to manage the risk of fluctuating carbon emission prices. These contracts are becoming increasingly prevalent as companies aim to reduce their carbon footprint. Conclusion Derivatives are complex financial instruments that can be beneficial or detrimental, depending on how they are used. They offer a range of uses in portfolio management, from managing risks to generating income. However, it is essential to understand the risks associated with each type of derivative and how they can be mitigated. With proper education and guidance, derivatives can be valuable tools in a well-diversified portfolio. As always, it is crucial to seek professional advice before incorporating any investment into your portfolio.

Chapter 17: Investment Analysis and Valuation

Fundamental and Technical Analysis

Investing in the financial market can be a daunting task for many, with constantly shifting news, market trends, and varying opinions from experts. This is where analysis and valuation techniques come into play. There are two main types of analysis that investors use to make informed decisions: fundamental and technical analysis. Fundamental analysis is a method of evaluating the intrinsic value of a security by analyzing economic and financial factors. It involves looking at a company's financial statements, industry trends, and overall economic conditions to determine the value of a stock. This type of analysis requires a deep understanding of the company and its business operations. On the other hand, technical analysis focuses on market data, such as price charts and trading volume, to predict future price movements. It assumes that the price of a security reflects all market information and trends, and analyzes historical patterns to forecast future trends. This type of analysis is more based on market psychology and the belief that patterns tend to repeat themselves. Both fundamental and technical analysis have their own strengths and limitations, and successful investors often use a combination of both to make informed decisions. Technical analysis can provide short-term insights, while fundamental analysis can help with long-term investment strategies.

Strategies for Valuation

Valuation is a crucial component of determining the attractiveness of an investment opportunity. It involves estimating the true worth of a security, such as a stock or a bond, and can help investors identify undervalued or overvalued assets. There are various strategies for valuation, and no single method is deemed to be the best. Instead, investors must understand the different approaches and choose the one that suits their investment goals. One common valuation strategy is the discounted cash flow (DCF) method, which uses projected future cash flows to estimate the current value of a security. Another approach is the price-to-earnings (P/E) ratio, which compares the current stock price to its earnings per share. This ratio can help investors determine if a stock is overvalued or undervalued compared to its industry peers. Another valuation strategy that is gaining popularity is the economic moat approach.

This method involves looking at a company's competitive advantages, or "moat," which can come in the form of unique products, cost advantages, or brand recognition. A strong moat can indicate a company's long-term sustainability and can help justify a higher valuation.

Case Studies

To understand the importance of investment analysis and valuation, let's look at some real-life case studies. In 2007, Warren Buffett's Berkshire Hathaway decided to invest $5 billion in Bank of America's preferred stock, which had an annual dividend of 6%. At the time, the stock was trading at a discount due to the financial crisis. Buffett saw this as an opportunity for a great investment and used fundamental analysis to determine the true value of the stock. Today, the investment is worth over $31 billion, proving the importance of proper valuation. Another famous case study is Tesla, a company that has seen a tremendous surge in its stock price in recent years. Tesla's stock surged over 800% in 2020, making it the largest global automaker by market cap. But what justified such a skyrocketing valuation?

Many analysts believe that it was a combination of both fundamental and technical analysis. While the company's financial statements showed strong potential for growth, the stock's momentum and market sentiment also played a significant role. Investment analysis and valuation are essential tools for any investor looking to make informed decisions and achieve their financial goals. By understanding the different types of analysis and valuation strategies, investors can take a more calculated approach to their investments and minimize their risk. Successful investors know that the key to success lies in proper analysis and thorough valuation, and having a well-rounded understanding of these concepts can help you make prudent investment decisions.

Chapter 18: Estate Planning for Business Owners

Succession Planning

As a business owner, you have dedicated countless hours and resources to building your company and ensuring its success. However, it is important to not only focus on the present, but also plan for the future. Succession planning is essential for the continued success of your business after you step down or pass away. One uncommon aspect of succession planning is finding the right successor. Many business owners assume that their children or family members will automatically be the best choice, but that is not always the case. It is important to consider the individual's skills, qualifications, and experience for the role. It may also be beneficial to seek outside help or guidance in identifying and preparing a successor. Another uncommon factor to consider is timing. While you may have an ideal timeline in mind for stepping down, unexpected events such as illness or a major market change could accelerate that timeline. It is important to have a plan in place for a smooth transition in case of such events.

Business Continuity

As a business owner, you have also built a successful and thriving company that provides for your employees and their families. Business continuity planning is crucial to ensure the survival of your business in the face of unforeseen events such as disasters, economic downturns, or sudden loss of key employees. One important aspect of business continuity planning is identifying and addressing potential risks. This could include reviewing insurance coverage, diversifying investments, or creating a crisis management plan. It is important to regularly reassess and update these plans as your business evolves and grows. Another uncommon factor to consider is the emotional impact on your employees. In the event of a sudden change in business ownership or structure, your employees may feel uncertain and anxious about the future. As a responsible business owner, it is important to consider their well-being and communicate openly and transparently about any changes or challenges.

Buy-sell Agreements

Buy-sell agreements are a key aspect of succession and continuity planning for businesses with multiple owners. These agreements outline what happens to a business in the event of a change in ownership or the departure of an owner, either voluntarily or involuntarily. One uncommon consideration for buy-sell agreements is considering the potential for disputes between owners. These agreements should clearly outline the process for resolving any conflicts and prevent the business from being negatively impacted. Another important factor to consider is the valuation of the business. Without a proper valuation, it can be difficult to determine a fair price for buying or selling shares. It is essential to regularly reassess the value of the business and update the buy-sell agreement accordingly. In conclusion, estate planning for business owners involves more than just considering how to transfer assets to the next generation. It also involves planning for the continued success and sustainability of the business. By incorporating succession planning, business continuity, and buy-sell agreements into your estate plan, you can protect your hard work and ensure the longevity of your business for future generations. Remember to regularly review and update these plans to reflect any changes in your business and personal circumstances.

Chapter 19: Wealth Management Strategies for Corporate and Executive Compensation

Types of Insurance

When it comes to wealth management for business owners, understanding the different types of insurance is crucial. Not only can insurance provide financial protection in times of unexpected events, but it can also play an important role in estate planning and tax management. Some commonly known types of insurance include life, health, and property insurance, but there are also less common types that can be beneficial for high-net-worth individuals. For example, key person insurance is a type of life insurance that protects a company in the event of a key employee's death. This can be especially important for small businesses that heavily rely on one or a few key employees for its success. Another type of insurance to consider is director and officer liability insurance, which protects key executives from personal liability in case of lawsuits related to their role in the company. When it comes to wealth management, insurance can serve as a safety net and provide peace of mind for both business owners and their families.

Assessing Risk

Assessing risk is a crucial part of wealth management for corporate and executive compensation. Risk can come in many forms, such as financial market volatility, lawsuits, and unexpected events. Without proper risk management, even the most successful businesses and individuals can suffer significant losses. One way to assess risk is through a thorough and regular review of financial statements, including income and expenses, assets and liabilities, and cash flow projections. This allows for a better understanding of the financial health of the business and can help identify potential areas of concern. In addition, it is important to conduct a risk assessment of the company's operations and identify any potential vulnerabilities. This can include identifying potential risks related to personnel, operations, and legal compliance. By proactively addressing and mitigating these risks, businesses can protect their assets and minimize potential losses.

Determining Coverage Needs

Once risks have been assessed, it is important to determine the appropriate coverage needs. This will depend on the specific needs and goals of the business and its executives. Working with a financial advisor or insurance specialist can help identify any potential gaps in coverage and ensure that the appropriate policies are in place. It is also important to regularly review and update insurance coverage as the business and its executives' needs change. As the business grows and evolves, so do the risks it faces. Additionally, major life events such as marriage, divorce, and the birth of children can also impact coverage needs. When determining coverage needs, it is important to consider not only the potential financial impact on the business and its executives, but also the implications and potential impact on their families and estate planning.

Uncommon Wealth Management Strategies for Corporate and Executive Compensation

In addition to traditional insurance policies, there are also some uncommon wealth management strategies that may be worth considering for corporate and executive compensation. One example is captive insurance, which is an insurance company owned by the insured business. This can provide more control and potentially greater tax benefits for the business compared to traditional insurance policies. Another strategy is utilizing cash value life insurance as a tool for tax-free retirement income and estate planning. It is also important to consider the tax implications of insurance policies. While premiums are typically not tax-deductible, the benefits received from insurance policies may have tax consequences. Working with a financial advisor and tax specialist can help navigate and optimize these potential tax implications.

In Conclusion

Wealth management for corporate and executive compensation involves much more than simply choosing insurance policies. It requires a comprehensive and proactive approach, assessing and managing risks, and determining coverage needs. By understanding the different types of insurance and considering uncommon wealth management strategies, business owners and executives can protect their assets, minimize risks, and achieve their financial goals.

Chapter 20: Alternative Investments

Chapter 20 delves into the world of alternative investments, exploring unique opportunities for wealth management in international markets. Through extensive research and expertise, Chartered Wealth Managers are equipped to assist their clients in navigating the complexities of alternative investments. With a focus on tax implications, currency risk, and asset allocation in global markets, this chapter will provide an in-depth understanding of this ever-evolving area of wealth management.

Tax Implications

One of the primary considerations when investing in international markets is the tax implications. Each country has its own tax laws and regulations, and it is crucial for wealth managers to have a deep understanding of these factors before advising clients on investments. For example, some countries may have favorable tax rates for certain types of investments, while others may have strict regulations that can impact returns. Therefore, it is important for Chartered Wealth Managers to have a global network of tax experts to ensure their clients' investments are optimized for tax benefits. Furthermore, as alternative investments can often be more complex than traditional investments, they may carry a higher tax burden. This could be due to various factors such as the type of investment, length of investment, or location. It is crucial for wealth managers to thoroughly assess and plan for potential tax implications to help their clients make informed investment decisions.

Currency Risk

In a global economy, currency risk is a prominent factor that must be considered when investing in international markets. Although exchange rates can fluctuate, foreign currency can present opportunities for diversified investment portfolios. Chartered Wealth Managers have the expertise to analyze currency trends and strategically allocate assets to minimize risks while taking advantage of potential gains. Uncommonly, alternative investments can also act as a hedge against currency risk. By investing in assets such as real estate or infrastructure in different countries, the returns can be decoupled from the home currency, reducing risk and providing stability in a portfolio.

Asset Allocation in Global Markets

Alternative investments, such as private equity, hedge funds, and commodities, provide opportunities for investor diversification. As the global market continues to evolve and grow, new investment trends and opportunities emerge. Chartered Wealth Managers have the expertise to navigate these markets and identify alternative investments that align with their clients' personal and financial goals. Moreover, asset allocation in global markets requires a deep understanding of cultural, economic, and political factors that may impact investment decisions. With a global perspective, wealth managers can advise their clients on a well-diversified portfolio that minimizes risk while maximizing potential returns.

In conclusion, alternative investments offer unique opportunities for wealth management in global markets. Tax implications, currency risk, and asset allocation are essential factors to be considered when exploring these investments. Through their expertise, Chartered Wealth Managers can guide their clients in making informed and strategic investment decisions to achieve their long-term financial goals.

Chapter 21: Introduction to Derivatives

Certificates of Deposits

When it comes to wealth management, investors are always on the lookout for low-risk and stable investment opportunities. One commonly overlooked option is certificates of deposit (CDs). These financial instruments are offered by banks and credit unions and provide a fixed interest rate for a fixed period of time, which could range from a few months to several years. What sets CDs apart from traditional savings accounts is their higher interest rates and guaranteed returns. While savings accounts may offer an interest rate of around 1%, CDs can provide rates as high as 2 to 3%. This makes them an attractive option for investors who are looking for a way to earn more on their savings without taking on too much risk. In addition to traditional CDs, there are also market-linked CDs that offer investors the potential for higher returns based on the performance of a specific market index. However, these may also come with a higher level of risk.

Municipal Bonds

Another popular investment option for wealth management clients is municipal bonds, also known as muni bonds. These are debt instruments issued by state or local governments to finance projects such as roads, schools, and hospitals. One of the main benefits of municipal bonds is their favorable tax treatment. The interest earned from muni bonds is usually exempt from federal taxes and may also be exempt from state and local taxes if the investor resides in the same state as the bond issuer. Municipal bonds also offer a high level of credit quality, as they are backed by the creditworthiness of the issuing government entity. This makes them a relatively safe investment option, but it's important to carefully research the credit ratings and financial stability of the issuer before investing.

Structured Notes

For investors looking for more complex and potentially high-yielding investment options, structured notes may be worth considering. These are debt securities that combine a bond component with a derivative component, often based on an underlying asset such as a stock or a commodity. The bond component of a structured note provides a fixed income stream, while the derivative component offers the possibility of a higher return based on the performance of the underlying asset. This combination makes structured notes a unique and potentially lucrative investment option. However, it's important for investors to understand the risks involved with structured notes, as they are complex financial products and may be difficult to liquidate. As with any investment, it's crucial to carefully research and fully understand the terms and risks before investing in structured notes.

Uncommon Investments to Consider

When it comes to wealth management, it's important for investors to have a diversified portfolio to help mitigate risk and potentially increase returns. While traditional options like stocks, bonds, and real estate are commonly utilized, there are also some more uncommon investments that may be worth considering. One option is rare collectibles, such as artwork or vintage cars, which can appreciate in value over time. For investors with a passion for a certain type of collectible, this could be a lucrative and enjoyable investment opportunity. Another option is peer-to-peer lending, which allows investors to lend money to individuals or businesses in exchange for a potentially higher interest rate than traditional savings accounts or bonds. However, it's important to carefully research the borrower's creditworthiness and potential risks before engaging in peer-to-peer lending. Cryptocurrencies, such as Bitcoin, are also gaining popularity as a potential investment option. However, these digital assets are highly volatile and present a higher risk of potential loss. Careful and thorough research is essential before investing in cryptocurrencies.

Wrapping Up

As a Chartered Wealth Manager, it is important to have a deep understanding of the various investment opportunities available to your clients. From traditional options like CDs and municipal bonds to more complex investments such as structured notes, there are a variety of ways to help your clients grow and protect their wealth. Remember to always consider your client's risk tolerance and long-term goals when making investment recommendations. And while it's important to stick to tried and true strategies, don't be afraid to explore and suggest uncommon investments that may align with your client's interests and provide potential for higher returns.

Chapter 22: Advanced Tax Planning Techniques

As a Chartered Wealth Manager (CWM), it is important to stay ahead of the game when it comes to tax planning. With constantly changing tax laws and regulations, it is crucial to utilize advanced techniques to help your clients maximize their wealth and minimize their tax burden. In this chapter, we will explore some uncommon, but highly effective, tax planning strategies that can set you apart as a CWM.

Hedging

Hedging is often associated with financial risk management, but it can also be used as a tax planning tool. It involves taking positions in financial instruments that are negatively correlated to the client's current investment holdings. This can provide a cushion against potential losses in the market and also help reduce tax liability. One of the lesser-known ways to use hedging for tax planning is through the use of put options. Put options give the holder the right to sell an underlying asset at a predetermined price, known as the strike price. If the market price of the asset falls below the strike price, the holder can exercise the option and sell the asset for a profit. This can be particularly useful for business owners who may have a large portion of their wealth tied up in their company's stock. By purchasing put options, business owners can protect themselves from potential losses and also use it as a tax-saving strategy.

Diversification

Diversification is a familiar concept for any CWM, but it can also be used as a tax planning technique. By diversifying a client's investment portfolio, you can spread out the tax liability over different asset classes and tax rates. This can help lower the overall tax burden and potentially save your clients thousands of dollars in taxes. One of the key benefits of diversification for tax planning is through the use of municipal bonds. Municipal bonds are issued by state and local governments and are exempt from federal income taxes. By incorporating these bonds into a client's portfolio, you can help reduce their taxable income and increase their after-tax return.

Rebalancing

Another vital aspect of wealth management is portfolio rebalancing. As a CWM, you must regularly review and adjust your client's investment portfolio to maintain the optimal asset allocation. This not only helps manage risk but can also be used as a tax planning strategy. In a traditional rebalancing approach, you would sell assets that have increased in value and use the proceeds to buy those that have decreased in value. However, this can trigger capital gains taxes for your clients. One way to mitigate this is through tax-loss harvesting. This involves selling assets that have incurred losses and using those losses to offset any gains in a client's portfolio. By implementing this strategy, you can reduce the client's overall tax liability while still maintaining the appropriate asset allocation. Some other advanced tax planning techniques that you can explore include using grantor retained annuity trusts (GRATs) and charitable remainder trusts (CRTs). GRATs allow individuals to transfer assets to future generations while minimizing the gift and estate taxes. CRTs, on the other hand, allow individuals to receive income from their assets during their lifetime while also receiving a charitable tax deduction. In the world of tax planning, there are always new and innovative strategies emerging. As a CWM, it is essential to continuously educate yourself and stay informed about these techniques to effectively serve your clients.

Conclusion

As we have seen, tax planning goes beyond simply minimizing tax liability on current income. It involves utilizing advanced techniques and strategies to strategically manage a client's wealth and reduce their overall tax burden. Hedging, diversification, and rebalancing are just a few ways that a CWM can use innovative practices to provide the best service to their clients. By staying informed and exploring uncommon methods, you can set yourself apart as a CWM and help your clients achieve their financial goals while maximizing their wealth. .

Chapter 23: Advanced Tax Planning Techniques

When it comes to wealth management, tax planning is a crucial aspect that cannot be overlooked. Not only can it help minimize your tax burden, but it can also have a significant impact on your overall financial plan. In this chapter, we will explore some advanced tax planning techniques that can take your wealth management strategy to the next level.

Giving Strategies

Charitable giving is a common practice among high-net-worth individuals, and for a good reason. Not only does it benefit the community, but it can also provide significant tax benefits. However, when it comes to giving, there are numerous strategies that can be employed to maximize the impact and tax benefits. One strategy is creating a donor-advised fund, which allows you to make a tax-deductible contribution to a charitable account and then distribute the funds to various charities over time. This provides the flexibility to support multiple causes while also receiving immediate tax benefits. Another strategy is utilizing a charitable remainder trust, where you can donate assets to the trust and receive an income stream for a set number of years. After the trust ends, the remaining assets are then donated to a designated charity, providing both income and tax benefits.

Impact Investing

Impact investing is a relatively new concept in the world of wealth management. It involves investing in companies or projects that have a positive social or environmental impact, alongside generating financial returns. This allows investors to align their values with their investments and make a meaningful contribution to causes they care about. One example of impact investing is investing in renewable energy projects. Not only does this support the transition to a more sustainable future, but it can also provide attractive financial returns. Impact investing allows investors to make a difference while also diversifying their portfolio and potentially reducing their tax burden.

Legacy Planning

Legacy planning goes beyond simply leaving assets for future generations. It involves crafting a lasting legacy that reflects your values, beliefs, and impact on the world. This can be achieved through various complex estate planning and tax strategies. For example, using a charitable lead trust allows you to donate assets to a charity for a set number of years while also providing a potential tax deduction. After the trust ends, the remaining assets are then passed on to your designated heirs. This not only supports a cause you care about but can also minimize estate tax burdens. Another technique is creating a family foundation, which allows you to involve your entire family in philanthropy and leave a lasting legacy. This provides a great opportunity to pass down your values to future generations while also supporting charitable causes. Incorporating legacy planning into your wealth management strategy can have a profound impact on your family and community for generations to come. Overall, advanced tax planning techniques can add a layer of complexity to wealth management. Therefore, it is essential to work closely with a qualified financial professional who has a deep understanding of tax laws and regulations. They can help you navigate through these strategies and create a tax-efficient plan that aligns with your goals and values. In this chapter, we have explored some uncommon but highly effective tax planning techniques, such as giving strategies, impact investing, and legacy planning. By incorporating these strategies into your wealth management plan, you can not only minimize your tax burden but also make a meaningful impact on society and leave a lasting legacy. As we move towards a more socially responsible and sustainable future, these strategies will continue to play a vital role in wealth management.

Chapter 24: Real Estate Investments

Real estate is a tried and true investment avenue, with many financial experts and entrepreneurs choosing to diversify their portfolios with this asset. It offers incredible long-term potential for growth and can provide a steady stream of passive income. In this chapter, we will explore the different types of real estate investments and their advantages and risks, as well as delve into the tax implications of such investments.

Types of Real Estate

When we think of real estate, the first thing that often comes to mind is residential properties. However, the real estate market is diverse and offers various types of investments. Some of the most common types of real estate investments include residential, commercial, industrial, and land. Residential properties refer to single-family homes, condos, townhouses, and multi-family properties. These types of investments are popular with first-time investors due to their perceived stability and ease of understanding. However, there is more to residential real estate investments than simply buying and renting out properties. Careful consideration must be given to factors such as location, property management, and tenant screening for success. Commercial properties, on the other hand, refer to buildings used for business purposes, such as office spaces, retail spaces, and warehouses. These types of investments often have long-term leases and higher rental incomes. However, they also come with higher expenses and a higher risk of vacancy. It is crucial to thoroughly research the market and the tenant before investing in commercial real estate. Industrial properties are also considered commercial real estate. These include properties used for manufacturing, distribution, and storage.

While these investments may not be as glamorous as their residential or commercial counterparts, they can offer significant returns, especially in growing markets. Lastly, land is another type of real estate investment that is often overlooked. Land can be purchased for future development, agriculture, or even as a recreational property. The price of land often increases as the population grows, making it a potentially valuable long-term investment.

Advantages and Risks

One of the main advantages of real estate investments is that they tend to be less volatile than other types of investments, such as stocks. They also offer the potential for steady passive income through rental properties. With careful research and management, real estate investments can also provide long-term growth and appreciation. However, like any investment, real estate also comes with risks. The market can fluctuate, and properties can remain vacant for extended periods, resulting in lost income. It is also essential to carefully manage expenses and factor in unexpected costs, such as repairs or legal fees. Additionally, the value of a property can decrease over time, making it a more long-term investment strategy. One uncommon risk in real estate investments is natural disasters. As the effects of climate change become more prevalent, investors must consider the location and potential hazards of a property before investing. Insurance can mitigate some risks, but thorough research and due diligence are essential in minimizing these risks.

Tax Implications

Real estate investments also come with various tax implications. One of the main benefits of investing in real estate is the ability to claim tax deductions on expenses related to the property. This includes mortgage interest, property taxes, and operating expenses. Depreciation can also be claimed on the property's value, reducing the owner's taxable income. However, there are also tax liabilities to consider when investing in real estate. Capital gains tax is applied when a property is sold at a profit, and rental income is also subject to taxation. 1031 exchanges, also known as like-kind exchanges, can defer capital gains tax when reinvesting the profits from a property sale into another investment property. As always, it is essential to consult with a tax professional to understand the specific tax implications of your real estate investments and plan accordingly. In conclusion, real estate investments offer tremendous potential for growth and passive income. The key to success in this asset class is thorough research, careful management, and a long-term investment approach. By diversifying your portfolio with real estate, you can achieve financial stability and work towards building a secure future.

Chapter 25: Advanced Wealth Management Strategies

Private Equity

Private equity has become an increasingly popular investment option in recent years, offering potentially high returns for those who are willing to take on more risk. For the uninitiated, private equity refers to investments made in private companies that are not listed on the stock market. This type of investment typically involves a significant amount of capital and a longer hold period compared to traditional stocks. However, this also means that investors have the potential to see even greater returns if the target company experiences exponential growth. One of the lesser-known aspects of private equity is the concept of "dry powder." This term refers to the amount of unspent capital that private equity firms have available to invest. In recent years, dry powder has reached record levels, with firms holding onto billions of dollars in cash. This can create a competitive environment for investors, as firms race to deploy their capital in the most strategic and profitable way possible.

Hedge Funds

Hedge funds are another investment option that may be worth considering for those who are looking to diversify their portfolio. These privately managed funds use a variety of strategies, including leveraging, derivatives, and short-selling, to potentially generate higher returns than traditional investments. However, with this potential for greater returns also comes higher risk. One of the lesser-known strategies used by hedge funds is called "activist investing." This involves taking a significant stake in a company and then using that influence to push for changes within the company, such as management or structural changes, in order to drive up the company's value. This can be a risky and controversial strategy, but it has the potential for substantial returns if successful.

Commodities

When discussing advanced wealth management strategies, commodities may not be the first thing that comes to mind. However, these tangible assets such as oil, gold, and agricultural products can offer diversification and potentially strong returns for investors. Commodities can also serve as a hedge against inflation, as their value tends to increase during times of economic uncertainty. One lesser-discussed aspect of commodities is their role in the global economy. For example, trading in crude oil not only affects investors but also has a significant impact on global politics and economies. Understanding these complex relationships and staying up-to-date on market trends can be crucial for successful commodity investing.

Art

While most people think of art as purely decorative, it can also be a valuable investment opportunity. The art market has been steadily growing in recent years, with record-breaking sales and high demand for rare and coveted pieces. Investing in art can provide diversification for portfolios that are heavily focused on traditional investments, such as stocks and bonds. One of the lesser-known aspects of art investing is the potential tax benefits. For example, in some countries, investing in certain types of art can provide significant tax breaks. This makes it an attractive option for high-net-worth individuals looking to minimize their tax liability.

Cryptocurrencies

Cryptocurrencies, such as Bitcoin and Ethereum, have been making headlines in recent years, causing many to wonder if they should be included in their investment portfolio. This digital form of currency operates independently of central banks and can offer high volatility, making it a potentially lucrative investment option. However, it also comes with a high level of risk, as the value of these currencies can fluctuate significantly. One aspect of cryptocurrencies that is not often discussed is the role they play in the future of technology. Blockchain, the underlying technology behind cryptocurrencies, has the potential to disrupt various industries, including finance, supply chain management, and voting systems. Keeping an eye on these developments can provide valuable insight into potential investment opportunities in this emerging market. In conclusion, advanced wealth management strategies can diversify and strengthen your portfolio, but they also come with higher risks. It's essential to thoroughly research and understand these options before investing and to regularly review and adjust your portfolio based on market conditions and your risk tolerance. By staying informed and continually educating yourself, you can make informed decisions that will help you achieve your financial goals.

Chapter 26: Advanced Tax Planning Techniques

Charitable Trusts

In the world of wealth management, charitable giving is often seen as an important aspect in creating a well-rounded financial plan. However, when it comes to advanced tax planning techniques, charitable trusts are an often overlooked option. Charitable trusts are a powerful tool that allows individuals to not only give back to their community, but also potentially reduce their overall tax burden. There are two types of charitable trusts – charitable lead trusts and charitable remainder trusts. The former allows individuals to make charitable contributions while still providing income for themselves or their beneficiaries. The latter, on the other hand, allows individuals to receive income from the trust for a certain amount of time, after which the remaining assets are then donated to their designated charities. One uncommon but effective strategy utilizing charitable trusts is the "clawback" approach. This involves setting up a charitable remainder trust and allowing the trustee to make distributions to the settlor until their passing. Upon their passing, the remainder of the assets is then distributed to the designated charities. This strategy not only allows individuals to receive income during their lifetime, but also provides a significant tax deduction for their estate upon their passing.

Donor-advised Funds

Another advanced tax planning technique in the realm of charitable giving is the use of donor-advised funds. This option combines the flexibility and control of a private foundation with the simplicity of a charitable giving fund. Donor-advised funds allow individuals to donate cash, securities, or other assets to a public charity, and recommend distributions to other charities of their choice. This approach can potentially provide significant tax deductions while also allowing individuals to have a say in where their charitable contributions go. One less common but effective strategy utilizing donor-advised funds is the "bunching" approach. This involves individuals bunching multiple years' worth of charitable contributions into one year, allowing them to itemize their deductions and potentially receive a larger tax benefit. They can then use a donor-advised fund to distribute the money to their selected charities over the course of several years.

Private Foundations

Private foundations are another advanced tax planning tool that can help individuals achieve their philanthropic goals while also reducing their tax burden. Private foundations are separate legal entities that are run by a board of directors and are funded by an individual, family, or corporation. These foundations allow individuals to have more control over their charitable giving, as they can choose the organizations they want to support and how the funds are distributed. One unique strategy utilizing private foundations is the use of philanthropic real estate. This involves donating a property to a private foundation, which then allows the organization to rent or sell the property and use the funds for charitable purposes. This not only provides tax benefits for the individual, but also creates a lasting source of income for the foundation. In conclusion, while charitable giving is often seen as a noble act, it can also be an effective tool for advanced tax planning. Charitable trusts, donor-advised funds, and private foundations offer individuals a way to make a positive impact in their community while also reducing their tax burden. As wealth management professionals, it is important to explore all the available options and find the best strategy for each individual client. With these advanced tax planning techniques, individuals can leave a lasting legacy while also securing their financial future.

Chapter 27: Disaster Planning, Cybersecurity, Estate Protection Strategies

While disaster planning and cybersecurity may seem like unlikely bedfellows in the world of wealth management, they are becoming increasingly important topics to address in light of the rising frequency of natural disasters and cyber attacks. Furthermore, estate protection strategies play a critical role in preserving wealth for future generations and ensuring a smooth transfer of assets.

Disaster Planning

The first topic in this chapter is disaster planning, which is a crucial aspect of any comprehensive wealth management strategy. Disasters, whether natural or man-made, can strike at any time and have a devastating impact on one's financial well-being. As such, it is imperative for wealth managers and their clients to discuss and plan for potential disasters. One uncommon aspect of disaster planning is the importance of considering geographical location. While it may seem obvious that areas prone to earthquakes, hurricanes, or wildfires should have tailored disaster plans, it is also essential to consider the potential impact of disasters on different types of assets. For example, a flood-prone area may not be suitable for a client with a valuable art collection. Therefore, it is crucial to have a comprehensive understanding of a client's assets and their vulnerability to potential disasters. Moreover, disaster planning should not only focus on mitigating financial losses but also on safeguarding the safety and well-being of clients and their families. Wealth managers should work closely with clients to develop emergency plans for evacuation, communication, and ensuring access to vital documents and assets in case of a disaster.

Cybersecurity

In today's digital age, cybersecurity is a paramount concern for individuals and businesses alike. As technology continues to advance, cyber threats are becoming more sophisticated and widespread, making it essential for wealth managers to address this issue with their clients. Uncommonly, wealth managers must educate clients on the various types of cyber threats, as well as ways to protect themselves from falling victim to scams, identity theft, or data breaches. This education should cover not only the basics of password protection and secure internet usage but also the potential risks associated with social media and public Wi-Fi networks. In addition to educating clients, wealth managers must also ensure the security of their own systems and data to protect their clients' sensitive information. This entails implementing stringent security protocols, regularly updating software and systems, and conducting thorough risk assessments.

Estate Protection Strategies

The final topic in this chapter is estate protection strategies, which are crucial for safeguarding one's wealth and ensuring a smooth transfer of assets to future generations. It involves creating a comprehensive plan for estate taxes, wills and trusts, and other legal considerations. An uncommon aspect of estate protection strategies is the incorporation of philanthropic giving into the plan. By setting up a charitable trust or foundation, individuals can both reduce their estate taxes and leave a lasting legacy by supporting causes close to their hearts. This strategy not only benefits the community but also provides a sense of fulfillment for the individual and their family. Furthermore, wealth managers must also consider potential family conflicts and challenges when developing estate protection strategies. Open and honest communication with all family members involved can help mitigate any issues and ensure a smooth transition of assets.

Conclusion

Disaster planning, cybersecurity, and estate protection strategies are three essential pillars of advanced wealth management. These topics may not initially seem interconnected, but they all play vital roles in preserving and protecting one's wealth. As such, wealth managers must address these issues with their clients and develop tailored strategies to mitigate risks and ensure financial stability for years to come.

Chapter 28: Advanced Portfolio Performance Measurement

Benchmarking

As a Chartered Wealth Manager, it is essential to not only measure the performance of your clients' portfolios, but also to compare it against a benchmark. A benchmark can be thought of as a point of reference or a standard against which the performance of a portfolio is measured. It provides a way to gauge how well the portfolio is performing in relation to the overall market or a specific asset class. While there are hundreds of benchmarks available, it is crucial to select the appropriate benchmark for each individual client's portfolio. This requires a thorough understanding of the portfolio's objectives, risk tolerance, and asset allocation. It is also essential to remember that benchmarks should be used as a tool for evaluation, not a goal. Be wary of chasing unrealistic benchmark returns, as it may lead to excessive risk-taking and potential losses for your clients.

Tracking Error

When discussing benchmarking, it is impossible not to mention tracking error. In simple terms, tracking error is a measure of how closely a portfolio mirrors its benchmark. A low tracking error indicates that the portfolio is closely following the benchmark, while a high tracking error could signal that the portfolio is actively deviating from the benchmark. While a low tracking error may seem desirable, it is essential to keep in mind that a portfolio's objective may not always align with the benchmark. As a CWM, your clients' objectives should be the primary focus, not simply tracking the benchmark. Additionally, a low tracking error does not necessarily equate to superior performance. A well-diversified portfolio with a slightly higher tracking error may provide better risk-adjusted returns in the long run.

Risk-adjusted Returns

Speaking of risk-adjusted returns, let's discuss the importance of this measurement.

This metric calculates returns taking into consideration the amount of risk taken to achieve those returns. As a CWM, it is crucial to not only focus on maximizing returns but to also manage risk. After all, wealth management is about preserving and growing your clients' wealth over time, not just chasing high returns that come with high risk. One of the commonly used risk-adjusted return measurements is the Sharpe ratio. It takes into account the portfolio's return, the risk-free rate, and the portfolio's volatility or standard deviation. A higher Sharpe ratio indicates that the portfolio is providing higher returns for the amount of risk taken compared to the risk-free rate.

Uncommon Practices in Performance Measurement

Now that we have covered the basics of performance measurement, let's discuss some lesser-known practices that can provide valuable insights into portfolio performance. One such practice is regression analysis. This method analyzes the relationship between the portfolio's returns and the returns of various asset classes, providing an understanding of how the portfolio is positioned in the market. It can also help identify any excessive exposure to a particular asset class. Another uncommon but useful practice is peer group analysis. This involves comparing a portfolio's performance against its peers within the same asset class or investment style. This can provide valuable insights into how well the portfolio is performing in relation to its peers and can help identify areas of improvement.

Embracing Technology for Performance Measurement

With the rapid advancements in technology, it is no surprise that the wealth management industry is also evolving. One significant change is the use of sophisticated software and tools for performance measurement. These tools can provide real-time data, detailed analysis, and customizable reporting for clients. As a CWM, embracing these technological advancements can help you stay efficient, accurate, and on top of your clients' portfolios' performance. It can also free up time for more valuable tasks such as client relationship management and financial planning.

The Ongoing Process of Performance Measurement

Finally, it is essential to remember that portfolio performance measurement is an ongoing process. It is not enough to measure performance and make decisions based on historical data. As a CWM, you must continuously monitor and evaluate the portfolio's performance, make adjustments when necessary, and communicate with your clients regularly. In conclusion, performance measurement is a critical aspect of wealth management, and as a CWM, it is your responsibility to ensure that your clients' portfolios are performing in line with their objectives. Utilizing benchmarks, tracking error, and risk-adjusted returns can provide valuable insights, but also remember to incorporate uncommon practices and embrace technology to stay ahead in the ever-evolving industry. Always remember that performance measurement is an ongoing process, and it requires diligence, attention to detail, and a client-focused approach.

Chapter 29: Client Education and Communication

As a Chartered Wealth Manager, one of your most important responsibilities is educating and communicating with your clients. After all, it is their hard-earned wealth that you are managing, and they deserve to understand the decisions being made on their behalf. In this chapter, we will delve deeper into the art of client education and communication, with a focus on understanding investor psychology, goal setting, and decision making.

Understanding Investor Psychology

To effectively educate and communicate with your clients, it is crucial to understand their psychological tendencies when it comes to investing. The field of behavioral finance has shown us that investors are not always rational, and emotions can significantly influence their decision-making process. Therefore, as a CWM, it is your job to be aware of these tendencies and help guide your clients towards more rational and informed decisions. One uncommon tendency to note is the "anchoring bias," where investors rely heavily on the first piece of information they receive, even if it is irrelevant to the current situation. This bias can lead to inaccurate expectations and ultimately affect the investment decisions made. As a CWM, you must reframe your clients' perspectives and guide them towards evidence-based decision making, rather than relying on preconceived notions or biases. Another crucial aspect of understanding investor psychology is recognizing the difference between risk tolerance and risk capacity. Risk tolerance refers to investors' emotional and psychological willingness to take on risk, while risk capacity is their financial ability to do so. As a CWM, it is your responsibility to assess both of these factors to create a suitable investment strategy for your clients.

Goal Setting

Before diving into investment decisions, it is essential to understand your clients' goals and objectives. A comprehensive goal-setting process includes not only financial goals but also personal and lifestyle goals. By taking a holistic approach to goal setting, you can create a customized and strategic plan for your clients, aligned with their values and priorities. Uncommonly, it is necessary to dig deeper into your clients' goals to uncover underlying motivations and potential obstacles. For example, your client may state that their financial goal is to retire in ten years. However, through further exploration, you may discover that their true goal is to travel extensively during retirement, and their biggest obstacle is their fear of running out of money. By understanding these underlying motivations and obstacles, you can better tailor your recommendations and address potential concerns, ultimately building trust and strengthening your client relationships. It is also important to revisit and reassess goals regularly. Life is constantly evolving, and goals may change accordingly. As a CWM, it is crucial to regularly review and adjust the investment strategy in line with your clients' goals and changing circumstances.

Decision Making

When it comes to making investment decisions, it is essential to involve your clients in the process. By regularly communicating and explaining the rationale behind investment decisions, you can foster a sense of ownership and partnership with your clients. This approach not only strengthens your client relationships, but it also helps them understand the potential risks and rewards of their investments. As a CWM, it is also your responsibility to mitigate any emotional biases that may affect decision making. This can include reframing your clients' perspectives, incorporating evidence-based research and analysis, and providing a long-term perspective rather than focusing on short-term fluctuations in the market. In addition to involving your clients in the decision-making process, it is equally important to communicate regularly with them. This includes providing updates on their investment performance, addressing any concerns or questions they may have, and educating them on any changes or developments in the market. By doing so, you can build trust and transparency with your clients, making them feel more confident and informed about their investment decisions.

In Conclusion

In this chapter, we have explored the art of client education and communication, with a focus on understanding investor psychology, goal setting, and decision making. As a CWM, it is crucial to not only have a deep understanding of these concepts but also be able to effectively apply them in your practice. By doing so, you can build strong and lasting relationships with your clients and help them achieve their financial goals and aspirations.

Chapter 30: The Future of Wealth Management

Family Values

In today's world, the concept of family values may seem antiquated or old-fashioned. However, for wealthy families, these values still hold a significant importance. When it comes to wealth management, it is crucial to understand and uphold the family's values to ensure a smooth and successful succession of wealth. These values may range from preserving family unity to maintaining a legacy of giving back to society. One important aspect of family values is the idea of stewardship. Wealth is not only about accumulating money and assets but also about preserving and managing them for future generations. It is essential to instill the sense of responsibility and duty in the heirs towards the family's wealth. By emphasizing stewardship, families can ensure that their legacy continues for generations to come.

Mission Statements

Mission statements are commonly associated with businesses, but they can also have a place in the world of wealth management. A mission statement is a concise statement that captures the essence of a person, family, or organization's goals and values. Creating a mission statement for the family's wealth can be a powerful tool for guiding the decision-making process and ensuring that the wealth is used in a way that aligns with the family's values. A well-crafted mission statement can also serve as a guiding principle for future generations. As the wealth is passed down, the mission statement can help the heirs understand the family's intentions and values. It can also serve as a reminder for them to stay true to those values when managing the wealth.

Next Generation Involvement

Traditionally, wealth management has been the domain of a select few, often leaving the next generation out of the picture entirely. However, in today's digital age, information and resources are more accessible than ever before. This means that the heirs of wealthy families are often more financially literate and tech-savvy than their predecessors. As wealth management evolves, it is essential to involve the next generation in the process. This involvement can go beyond simply educating them on financial matters. It can also involve giving them a seat at the table and allowing them to have a say in the family's wealth management decisions. By involving the next generation, families can ensure that their legacy and values are carried on and adapted as time goes on.

Uncommon Perspectives

As with any profession, it is easy to get stuck in one's routine and way of thinking. However, in wealth management, it is crucial to step back and consider unconventional perspectives and ideas from time to time. This could mean thinking outside the box when it comes to investment strategies, considering innovative ways to give back to society, or even involving a diverse range of voices in the decision-making process. By embracing uncommon perspectives, families and wealth managers can tap into new ideas and approaches that could lead to greater success and growth. Additionally, it can also help keep wealth management interesting and exciting, preventing it from becoming stagnant and outdated.

Conclusion

The world of wealth management is constantly evolving, and as we look to the future, it is essential to consider the role of family values, mission statements, and next-generation involvement. By upholding family values, creating a mission statement, involving the next generation, and embracing uncommon perspectives, families can ensure that their wealth continues to grow and support future generations. Wealth management is not just about managing assets; it is about preserving a family's legacy and values. As we move forward, let us remember that wealth, in all its forms, is a precious and powerful tool for creating a positive impact on the world.

Chapter 31: Financial Planning for Business Owners

Maximizing Business Value

As a business owner, your main goal is to create a successful and profitable company. However, many business owners neglect to consider how their business can contribute to their overall wealth plan. Maximizing the value of your business is crucial for long-term financial stability and growth. Here are some uncommon things to keep in mind when it comes to maximizing business value:

- Diversify Your Business: While having a niche market may have helped your business initially, relying on one specific product or service may limit your potential for growth and value. Diversifying your offerings can attract a wider customer base and increase the value of your business.

- Invest in Technology: With the constantly evolving technological landscape, it's important to stay ahead of the game. Investing in the latest technology can not only improve your business operations but also show potential buyers that your business is modern and adaptable.

- Utilize Strategic Partnerships: Partnering with other businesses can not only increase your reach and customer base but also add value to your company. Seek out partnerships that align with your business goals and values to create a mutually beneficial relationship.

- Have a Succession Plan: It's important to think about the long-term future of your business, even if you're not planning on selling anytime soon. Having a succession plan in place ensures a smooth transition and can add value to your business in the eyes of potential buyers.

Building Wealth Outside the Business

While your business is likely a major source of your wealth, it's important to not put all your eggs in one basket. Building wealth outside of your business can provide financial security and diversification. Some ways to do this include:

- Personal Investments: Consider diversifying your investments outside of your business. This can include stocks, real estate, or other alternative investments. Consult with a financial advisor to determine the best investment strategy for your individual goals and risk tolerance.

- Retirement Planning: As a business owner, you don't have the luxury of a company-provided retirement plan. It's crucial to have a solid retirement plan in place to ensure a comfortable future. Consider options such as a SEP IRA, Solo 401(k), or Defined Benefit Plan.

- Life Insurance: In addition to providing financial protection for your loved ones, life insurance can also be a valuable asset in building wealth. A cash value life insurance policy can provide a tax-free source of income in retirement and can also be used as collateral for business loans.

- Philanthropy: Giving back to causes you care about is not only personally fulfilling, but it can also provide tax benefits and contribute to your overall legacy. Consider incorporating charitable giving into your overall financial plan. Business owners have a unique set of challenges and opportunities when it comes to wealth management.

By effectively managing your business and building wealth outside of it, you can create a strong foundation for long-term financial success. Don't underestimate the importance of including your business in your overall financial plan, and make sure to regularly reassess and adjust as your business and personal goals evolve.

Chapter 32: Investment Strategies in Retirement

Asset Allocation

When it comes to retirement planning, one of the most important things to consider is asset allocation. This refers to the process of spreading your investments across different asset classes such as stocks, bonds, and cash, in order to manage risk and potentially increase returns. However, when it comes to retirement, your focus should shift from wealth accumulation to wealth preservation. This means that having a well-balanced and diversified portfolio becomes even more crucial. Retirees often make the mistake of being too conservative with their investments, which can lead to insufficient returns and being unable to keep up with inflation. On the other hand, being too aggressive can also be risky and potentially lead to losing a significant portion of your savings. Therefore, it is important to work with a CWM and find the right balance based on your risk tolerance, time horizon, and financial goals. In addition to traditional asset classes, retirees should also consider alternative investments, such as real estate, private equity, and hedge funds. These investments can offer diversification and potentially higher returns, but also usually come with higher risk. It is essential to work with an experienced CWM to determine if alternative investments are suitable for your retirement portfolio.

Generating Income

One of the main concerns for retirees is generating a reliable and sustainable stream of income. With the decline in traditional pension plans and the uncertainty of Social Security, it is crucial to have a well-thought-out retirement income plan. This includes understanding different income sources such as Social Security benefits, retirement accounts, dividends, and interest income from investments. In addition to these traditional sources, retirees should also explore alternative ways of generating income. This can include rental properties, annuities, and dividends from REITs (Real Estate Investment Trusts). Working with a CWM can help you determine the best income-generating strategy for your retirement, taking into account your financial goals and risk tolerance.

Long-term Care Considerations

It is estimated that 70% of people over the age of 65 will require some form of long-term care in their lifetime. This can be a significant financial burden for retirees, and therefore, it is important to plan for this potential expense. This includes exploring long-term care insurance, which can cover the costs of nursing homes, assisted living facilities, and home care. Long-term care insurance is not a one-size-fits-all solution and can be costly. It is essential to work with a CWM to determine if this insurance is right for you and your retirement plan. There are also new hybrid policies available that combine long-term care insurance with life insurance or annuities, which can offer more flexibility and potentially lower premiums. Another important consideration related to long-term care is estate planning. As part of your estate plan, you can designate a healthcare power of attorney and outline your preferences for end-of-life care. This ensures that your wishes are followed and can also help your family avoid legal battles and financial strain.

Conclusion

Retirement planning is a complex and ever-evolving process that requires careful consideration and professional guidance. As a CWM, our goal is to help you achieve your retirement goals and enjoy your golden years with financial security. By taking a holistic approach to investment strategies in retirement, considering asset allocation, generating income, and long-term care considerations, we can create a personalized plan that is tailored to your unique needs and goals. With the right strategy and firm understanding of all your options, you can confidently embark on your retirement journey.

Chapter 33: Advanced Tax Planning Techniques

As a Chartered Wealth Manager (CWM), it is crucial to stay up-to-date with the constantly evolving tax laws and strategies. In this chapter, we will explore some unconventional and innovative ways to help clients minimize their tax burden and maximize their wealth.

Charitable Gifting Strategies

Charitable giving is not only a noble act but also a powerful tax planning tool. As a CWM, it is essential to educate your clients about the various ways they can make charitable donations while also receiving tax benefits. One strategy that is gaining popularity is the Donor Advised Fund (DAF). With a DAF, clients can make a lump-sum donation to a charitable organization and receive an immediate tax deduction. The donated funds can then be invested and grow tax-free, allowing clients to distribute funds to chosen charities at their discretion. Another effective strategy is the use of a Charitable Remainder Trust (CRT). With a CRT, clients can donate appreciated assets to a trust, receive an immediate tax deduction, and receive annual payments from the trust for a specified time. At the end of the trust's term, the remaining assets are donated to the designated charity. This strategy not only provides tax benefits but also allows clients to receive income from the donated assets.

Tax-loss Harvesting

Tax-loss harvesting is a technique that involves strategically selling investments at a loss to offset capital gains in a portfolio. This strategy is especially useful in volatile markets, where it is common to see a mix of both gains and losses. By selling investments at a loss, clients can reduce their tax liability while still maintaining their desired asset allocation. However, it's not enough to sell investments at a loss. CWMs must also consider the wash-sale rule, which prohibits investors from claiming a loss on a security if they repurchase it within 30 days. To avoid this, CWMs can help their clients make a similar but not identical investment to maintain their market exposure while still claiming the loss for tax purposes.

Tax-efficient Withdrawal Strategies

Now, let's talk about tax-efficient withdrawal strategies for retirement accounts. As a CWM, it's crucial to develop a plan that minimizes the tax impact for your clients as they take distributions from their retirement accounts. One effective strategy is the "bucket approach," where clients have different buckets for different types of investments, such as taxable accounts and retirement accounts. By withdrawing funds strategically from each bucket, clients can minimize their tax liability, especially if they have enough time before required minimum distributions (RMDs). Clients can also benefit from the "Roth conversion" strategy. With a Roth conversion, clients can convert funds from a traditional IRA to a Roth IRA, paying taxes on the converted amount at their current tax rate. This strategy can be especially beneficial for clients in a lower tax bracket, as they can take advantage of lower tax rates now and potentially avoid higher tax rates in the future.

Uncommon Strategies in Tax Planning

As CWMs, it's vital to think outside the box and explore unconventional strategies to help clients minimize their taxes. One such strategy is "income shifting," where high-income earners can shift income to their children or other family members in lower tax brackets. This can be achieved through gifts, loans, or hiring family members for work. Another uncommon but effective strategy is "bunching deductions." Taxpayers can bunch deductions in certain years, such as doubling up on charitable donations or property tax payments, to exceed the standard deduction and reduce their taxable income. They can then take the standard deduction in other years, therefore, reducing their overall tax liability.

Conclusion

In conclusion, as a CWM, it is crucial to stay on top of advanced tax planning techniques to help your clients build and preserve their wealth. By exploring charitable gifting strategies, tax-loss harvesting, and tax-efficient withdrawal strategies, along with uncommon strategies, you can provide your clients with a comprehensive and sophisticated approach to minimize their tax burden. Remember, every client's financial situation is unique, so it's essential to tailor your strategies to their specific needs and goals.

Chapter 34: Advanced Estate Planning Techniques

Setting Up and Managing a Family Office

As families amass significant wealth, they often look for ways to keep their assets secure and ensure that future generations are taken care of. One option that has gained popularity in recent years is setting up a family office. A family office is a private wealth management advisory firm that is solely dedicated to managing the financial affairs of a wealthy family. It can offer a range of services, including investment management, tax planning, and estate planning, tailored to the specific needs of the family. Setting up a family office requires careful consideration and planning. It is not just about managing money, but also about managing family dynamics and relationships. One of the key benefits of a family office is that it can provide a centralized approach to managing the family's wealth, which can help to avoid conflict and facilitate transparency. It can also provide a sense of continuity for future generations, ensuring that the family's legacy and values are preserved. There are two main types of family offices - single-family and multi-family.

A single-family office is solely dedicated to managing the financial affairs of one family. In contrast, a multi-family office serves multiple families, providing a range of services for a fee. Single-family offices tend to have more control over the management of the family's wealth, but they also come with a higher cost. Managing a family office requires a team of skilled professionals, including lawyers, financial advisors, tax specialists, and estate planners. These professionals work together to develop a comprehensive financial plan that aligns with the family's goals and values. They are also responsible for implementing and monitoring the plan, ensuring that the family's assets are managed in a tax-efficient manner and that the overall strategy is reviewed and updated regularly. Succession planning is a crucial aspect of managing a family office. It involves identifying who will take over the management of the family office when the current generation steps down or passes away. This involves not only selecting the right individuals but also providing them with the necessary training and guidance to ensure a smooth transition.

Succession Planning

Effective succession planning involves considering all aspects of the family business and wealth. It is not just about identifying a successor, but also about developing a clear process for transitioning leadership and wealth management responsibilities. This process should be well-thought-out and communicated to all family members, ensuring transparency and addressing any potential conflicts. Succession planning can also involve creating a governance framework that outlines roles, responsibilities, and decision-making processes within the family office. This is especially important when there are multiple family members involved in the management of the family's wealth. It can help to prevent disagreements and misunderstandings by providing a clear structure for decision-making.

Another crucial aspect of succession planning is developing a training and development plan for family members who will take on leadership roles in the family office. This ensures that they have the necessary skills, knowledge, and experience to manage the family's wealth effectively. It can also help to instill the family's values and ensure that they are passed down to future generations. A successful succession plan also takes into account potential risks and unforeseen events. This can include disability or death of key family members involved in the family office. Having contingency plans in place for such situations can help to ensure a smooth transition and minimize disruptions to the family's wealth management. In conclusion, setting up and managing a family office requires thorough planning, careful consideration, and regular review. It is not just about managing financial assets but also about preserving a family's legacy and values. With a proper governance structure, effective succession planning, and a team of skilled professionals, a family office can provide significant benefits for future generations to come.

Irrevocable Trusts: A Powerful Tool for Wealth Preservation

Many people are familiar with the concept of a trust, where a person (the trustee) holds and manages assets on behalf of another person (the beneficiary). However, irrevocable trusts take this concept to the next level. Unlike revocable trusts, where the grantor can make changes at any time, irrevocable trusts cannot be modified or terminated after they are created. This might sound concerning, but it is precisely why irrevocable trusts are so powerful for wealth preservation. One of the main benefits of irrevocable trusts is that they remove assets from the grantor's estate, thus reducing the potential estate taxes. This is especially useful for individuals with a high net worth who want to pass on their wealth to their loved ones without incurring huge tax liabilities. Additionally, since the assets are held by the trust and not owned by the beneficiaries, they are protected from creditors, lawsuits, and other potential threats. Another uncommon but vital aspect of irrevocable trusts is its ability to protect assets from the costs of long-term care. As we age, the costs of healthcare and long-term care can significantly impact our wealth. With an irrevocable trust, the assets technically belong to the trust, and therefore, are not counted towards Medicaid eligibility. This can be immensely helpful in preserving assets and providing for your loved ones' long-term care needs.

Grantor Retained Annuity Trusts (GRATs): Passing on Wealth Tax Efficiently

A Grantor Retained Annuity Trust (GRAT) is an estate planning tool designed to transfer assets to future generations while minimizing the tax liability. It allows the grantor to transfer assets into the trust while retaining an annuity payment for a set period. After that period, the remaining assets in the trust are transferred to the beneficiaries. One of the main advantages of GRATs is its potential for tax savings. Since the grantor retains the annuity payment, the value of the assets transferred is reduced, and thus, the gift tax liability is also reduced. Additionally, if the assets in the trust appreciate at a rate higher than the IRS's prescribed interest rate, the grantor can transfer even more wealth to the beneficiaries with minimal tax consequences. GRATs are also valuable for family business owners who want to pass on their business to the next generation. By transferring shares of the business to a GRAT, the grantor can gradually transfer ownership while also generating income for themselves. This can be especially useful for business owners who want to retire but still want to maintain some control over the business.

Family Limited Partnerships: Managing Wealth and Protecting Family Legacy

A Family Limited Partnership (FLP) is a legal structure that allows family members to pool their assets and create a family business entity. It involves two types of partners:

general partners (typically parents) who manage the partnership and limited partners (typically children) who contribute assets. The limited partners can receive distributions from the partnership, but they do not have control over the assets. FLPs are primarily used for estate planning purposes, with the main goal being to transfer wealth to the next generation while preserving the family legacy. By transferring assets into the partnership, the parents can reduce the value of their estate and potentially minimize estate taxes. Additionally, since the limited partners have no control over the assets, they are protected from potential lawsuits or creditors. Another uncommon but crucial use of FLPs is facilitating family communication and management of assets. By creating a structure where family members have a role to play, it encourages communication, cooperation, and accountability. Additionally, parents can use this as a tool to teach financial responsibility and management skills to their children. In conclusion, advanced estate planning techniques such as irrevocable trusts, GRATs, and family limited partnerships offer a world of possibilities for high net-worth individuals. These tools not only help minimize tax liabilities but also provide protection and control over assets. As with any estate planning strategy, it is crucial to work with a qualified and experienced professional to ensure that these techniques are implemented properly to meet your goals and objectives.

Chapter 35: Corporate and Executive Compensation

When we think of corporate and executive compensation, the first thing that may come to mind are large bonuses, fancy perks, and luxurious lifestyles. While these may be a part of the picture, there is a much more complex and nuanced world behind executive compensation that is rarely talked about. In this chapter, we will dive into the details of equity-based compensation, employee benefits, and the tax implications that come with these forms of compensation.

Equity-based Compensation

Equity-based compensation refers to any type of employee pay that includes ownership in the company. This can come in the form of stock options, restricted stock units, or performance-based grants. One of the most common forms of equity-based compensation is stock options, where employees are given the right to purchase company stock at a predetermined price in the future. This can be a valuable way for executives to have a stake in the success of the company and be rewarded for their contributions. However, there are some uncommon things to consider when it comes to equity-based compensation. For example, there may be restrictions on when the stock options can be exercised, such as a vesting period or certain performance goals that need to be met. It's important for executives to fully understand the terms and conditions of their equity-based compensation to avoid any unexpected surprises.

Employee Benefits

Employee benefits are another important aspect of corporate and executive compensation. These can include health insurance, retirement plans, and other perks like company cars or gym memberships. These benefits not only serve as incentives for employees to stay with the organization, but they also play a crucial role in attracting top talent in a competitive job market. One uncommon consideration when it comes to employee benefits is the non-financial impact they can have. For example, offering a comprehensive health insurance plan can improve employee morale and well-being, leading to increased productivity and loyalty. Companies should carefully evaluate and tailor their benefits packages to meet the needs and values of their employees.

Tax Implications

The tax implications of corporate and executive compensation can be complex and require careful planning. One important aspect to consider is the tax rate for different types of compensation. For example, while cash bonuses are subject to income tax, equity-based compensation may be subject to capital gains tax when the employee decides to sell the stock. Another uncommon consideration when it comes to taxes and executive compensation is the impact on the company's overall bottom line. For publicly traded companies, executive compensation packages are often disclosed in regulatory filings and can come under scrutiny from shareholders and the public. It's important for companies to strike a balance between offering attractive compensation packages to top executives while also being mindful of how it may be perceived by stakeholders. In addition, there are various tax strategies that can be employed to minimize the tax burden for both the company and the executive. For example, using a deferred compensation plan can allow executives to defer receiving income until a later date when they may be in a lower tax bracket.

These strategies require careful planning and implementation by a team of experienced tax and financial professionals. While corporate and executive compensation may seem like a straightforward concept, there are many uncommon considerations that need to be taken into account. From equity-based compensation to employee benefits and tax implications, it takes a comprehensive and strategic approach to effectively manage and optimize executive compensation plans. As the landscape of corporate governance and societal expectations continue to evolve, it's important for companies to continue reevaluating and updating their compensation strategies to align with the needs and values of their executives and employees.

Chapter 36: Estate Transfer and Preservation

Estate transfer and preservation is a crucial aspect of wealth management. As we look into the different strategies for managing this process, we must consider the impact on not only our clients but also their families and their legacies. In this chapter, we will explore some uncommon yet impactful strategies for estate tax planning, life insurance, and business succession planning.

Estate Tax Strategies

Estate taxes can take a significant chunk out of a person's wealth, and it is essential to develop a strategy to minimize the impact. While the use of trusts, gifting, and life insurance are common methods, there are also some uncommon strategies that can be employed. One such strategy is the use of a grantor-retained annuity trust (GRAT). A GRAT allows the grantor to transfer assets to the trust while retaining the right to receive an annuity payment for a set period. This allows the appreciation of the trust assets to pass to the beneficiaries without being subject to estate tax. Another strategy is creating a Family Limited Partnership (FLP). An FLP allows for the transfer of assets to the partnership, which is then owned by family members. By doing so, the assets are removed from the individual's estate and can be transferred to heirs at a lower tax rate.

Life Insurance

Life insurance is often used as a tool for estate planning, especially when it comes to providing for loved ones after an individual's passing. However, life insurance can also be utilized in unique and creative ways for wealth preservation. One such strategy is the use of a Life Insurance Trust (ILIT). By placing a life insurance policy in trust, the proceeds can be kept out of the individual's estate and therefore not subject to estate taxes. It also allows for greater control over the distribution of the proceeds to beneficiaries. Another interesting approach is the use of an irrevocable life insurance trust (ILIT) for charitable giving. By transferring a life insurance policy to an ILIT, the premium payments can be used as a charitable tax deduction. It allows for philanthropy while still providing for loved ones.

Business Succession

Planning For business owners, succession planning is crucial to ensure the smooth transition of ownership and management when they retire or pass away. While there are many common approaches to this, there are also some unconventional methods that can be beneficial. One such strategy is using an Employee Stock Ownership Plan (ESOP). An ESOP allows business owners to transfer ownership of the company to its employees, providing them with a stake in the business's success. It also offers tax benefits for both the business and the owner. Another option is a Qualified Personal Residence Trust (QPRT), which allows business owners to transfer their primary residence to a trust and continue living in it for a set period. After that time, the trust transfers ownership of the property to the designated beneficiaries, resulting in reduced estate taxes. In conclusion, estate transfer and preservation require careful planning and consideration of not only the financial implications but also the emotional impact on the individual and their loved ones. As CWMs, it is our duty to educate and guide our clients through these decisions and offer creative and unique solutions to achieve their desired outcomes. By utilizing some of the lesser-known strategies discussed in this chapter, we can help our clients preserve their wealth and leave a lasting legacy for future generations.

Chapter 37: Wealth Transfer and Preservation

Making an Impact

When it comes to wealth management, many think solely in terms of financial growth and preservation. However, as a Chartered Wealth Manager, it is important to consider the impact your clients' wealth can have on their family and community for generations to come. In this chapter, we will delve into the importance of philanthropy and family legacy planning in wealth management. By incorporating these elements into your clients' financial plans, you can make a lasting impact on their lives and the lives of others. Philanthropy is about more than just donating money to charities; it is about creating a positive change in the world. As a CWM, you have the opportunity to help your clients identify causes that align with their values and passions, and create a strategic giving plan to make a difference in those areas. By involving your clients' families in philanthropy, you can also instill important values and lessons in the younger generations. This can not only bring families closer together, but also create a legacy of generosity and social responsibility.

Screening Strategies

When it comes to philanthropic giving, it is important to not only choose the right causes, but also the right organizations. As a CWM, you have the expertise to research and analyze various charities and non-profits to ensure that your clients' donations are making a real impact. Some key factors to consider when screening potential organizations include their mission, transparency, financial stability, and track record of success. You can also look into their resources and partnerships to see if they are effectively using their funds and making a difference in the communities they serve. Additionally, you may want to consider socially responsible investments for your clients who are interested in aligning their values with their financial goals. These investments focus on companies or sectors that are making a positive impact on the environment or society.

Performance Analysis

Like any aspect of wealth management, measuring the performance of philanthropic endeavors is crucial for success. This not only keeps your clients accountable for their giving, but also allows you to track the impact of their contributions. Performance analysis can include metrics such as number of people helped, dollars donated, and tangible outcomes achieved. However, it is also important to consider the qualitative impact, such as the change in community attitudes or the shift in the lives of those affected by the organization. Through performance analysis, you can also identify any areas for improvement or opportunities for your clients to get more involved with the charities they support. This can lead to more meaningful and impactful philanthropy for your clients and their families. In conclusion, wealth transfer and preservation involves much more than just financial planning. As a CWM, you have the ability to help your clients create a legacy of generosity and social responsibility through strategic philanthropy and family legacy planning. By incorporating these elements into your clients' financial plans, you can truly make a lasting impact on the world.

Chapter 38: The Future of Wealth Management

We live in a constantly evolving world, and the same applies to the world of wealth management. As we move further into the future, new technologies, socio-economic factors, and market changes will shape the landscape of wealth management. As a Chartered Wealth Manager, it is important to stay ahead of the game and be prepared for what lies ahead. In this chapter, we will explore some of the trends and factors that will impact the future of wealth management.

Market Updates

The financial market is always in a state of flux, and it is essential for wealth managers to stay updated on the latest developments. In the future, the financial market is expected to become even more globalized and interconnected. As a result, wealth managers will need to have a deeper understanding of international markets and be able to navigate volatile market conditions with ease. Additionally, the rise of new technologies such as artificial intelligence and blockchain will have a significant impact on the financial market. These technologies have the potential to revolutionize the way we manage investments and make financial decisions. Wealth managers will need to adapt and incorporate these technologies into their strategies to stay competitive.

Financial Literacy

Financial literacy is a vital aspect of wealth management, and it is something that will become increasingly important in the future. As the younger generation becomes more involved in managing their wealth, it is essential for wealth managers to educate and empower them to make informed financial decisions. It is also crucial for wealth managers to recognize the importance of financial literacy for their clients. Many people do not have a thorough understanding of financial concepts and products, which can lead to confusion and mismanagement of their wealth. In the future, it will be vital for wealth managers to not only manage their clients' wealth but also educate and empower them to make sound financial decisions.

Educational Events

In the fast-paced world we live in, it can be challenging to stay updated on the latest developments in the financial industry. However, educational events and conferences provide an excellent opportunity for wealth managers to gain knowledge, network with peers, and stay updated on the latest trends. In the future, we can expect to see a significant increase in the number and variety of educational events and conferences for wealth managers. These events will not only focus on traditional topics such as investments and risk management but also touch on emerging technologies and socio-economic trends. They will act as a platform for wealth managers to exchange ideas, learn from experts, and gain a deeper understanding of the evolving landscape of wealth management.

Uncommon Things to keep in mind

As a wealth manager, it is crucial to think beyond the traditional approaches and strategies. Keeping an open mind and considering uncommon factors can give you an edge and set you apart from other wealth managers. One uncommon factor to keep in mind is the significance of digital assets. With the rise of cryptocurrencies and other digital assets, wealth managers will need to have a comprehensive understanding of these assets and how to incorporate them into their clients' portfolios. Another factor to consider is the impact of climate change on wealth management. As the world becomes more environmentally conscious, investors are increasingly looking for socially responsible and sustainable investment options. In the future, wealth managers will need to incorporate these factors into their strategies to retain clients and attract new ones.

In conclusion

The future of wealth management is exciting and full of opportunities, but it also comes with its challenges. As a Chartered Wealth Manager, it is crucial to be adaptable, open-minded, and constantly learning. By staying updated, educating and empowering clients, and considering uncommon factors, you can thrive in the ever-changing world of wealth management.

Book 2 - Ethical and Regulatory Framework

Chapter 1: The World of Chartered Wealth Management

The Evolving Role of a CWM In today's fast-paced world, where financial decisions and investments can make or break a person's future, the need for a skilled and knowledgeable wealth manager has never been more crucial. This is where a Chartered Wealth Manager (CWM) comes into play. With the changing dynamics of the finance industry, the role of a CWM has evolved significantly, making it a highly sought-after profession for those with a passion for finance and a talent for strategic planning.

Role of a CWM

The role of a CWM goes far beyond managing wealth and investments for clients. A CWM is a trusted advisor, responsible for ensuring financial stability and security for clients through sound financial planning and risk assessment. The focus of a CWM is not just on the current financial situation of their clients, but also on their future financial goals, such as retirement planning, education planning, and legacy planning. In addition to providing financial guidance, a CWM also acts as a mentor, helping clients make informed and strategic decisions that align with their financial objectives. This involves understanding the client's risk tolerance, investment goals, and overall financial situation to develop a customized financial plan that fits their needs. A CWM's role also includes regularly monitoring and rebalancing investment portfolios to ensure they align with the client's goals and risk tolerance.

Job Opportunities

As the finance industry continues to grow and evolve, the demand for skilled wealth managers is also increasing. This presents a plethora of job opportunities for those in pursuit of a career in finance, specifically in wealth management. Holding a CWM designation is highly regarded and opens doors to various job opportunities in private banking, wealth management firms, financial planning firms, and even consulting firms. Moreover, with the growth of technology and the rise of virtual wealth management platforms, CWMs can now also offer their services globally, expanding their potential client base.

Importance in the Finance Industry

In the finance industry, where trust and credibility are of utmost importance, a CWM designation holds great significance. Earning a CWM designation not only demonstrates an individual's expertise and knowledge in wealth management but also their commitment to upholding ethical and professional standards. This is crucial in an industry where clients entrust their financial security and future to the guidance of their wealth manager. Moreover, with the changing landscape of the finance industry, the CWM designation has become a symbol of adaptability and continuous professional development. CWMs are required to undergo continuing education and stay updated with the latest market trends and investment strategies, enabling them to provide the best possible advice and results for their clients.

Uncommon Insights

One of the lesser-known facts about CWMs is that they are not just limited to managing wealth for high net worth individuals. While their expertise is highly sought after by wealthy individuals, CWMs can also serve as valuable resources for individuals with various income levels. This highlights the reach and impact of a CWM in promoting financial stability and security for all individuals, regardless of their financial status. Another interesting aspect of the CWM designation is the global recognition it holds. CWMs are part of an international community of finance professionals, allowing for knowledge sharing and networking opportunities. This also means that CWMs can provide their services to clients globally, further strengthening the importance and relevance of the designation in the finance industry.

The Changing Landscape

The finance industry is constantly evolving and adapting to new market trends and technological advancements. This also means that the role of a CWM will continue to evolve and expand, making it an exciting and dynamic field for aspiring wealth managers. As the world becomes more interconnected and global, the demand for skilled CWMs will only continue to increase, highlighting the importance and value of this designation in the finance industry.

History

The roots of wealth management can be traced back to the early 20th century when banks and financial institutions started offering specialized services to cater to the needs of wealthy clients. However, it wasn't until the 1970s that the term "wealth management" was first used by US bankers and financial planners. During this time, the industry experienced a rapid growth phase, fueled by the rising number of high-net-worth individuals (HNWI) and their complex financial needs. The 1990s saw a significant shift in the wealth management landscape as traditional banks and independent advisors faced competition from new market entrants such as private banks and multi-family offices. The rise of globalization and digitalization also played a crucial role in shaping the industry, making it easier for individuals to access wealth management services and invest globally.

Growth

The wealth management industry has seen impressive growth over the last few decades. According to the 2020 World Wealth Report by Capgemini, global high-net-worth individual wealth reached a record high of $74 trillion in 2019, a 9.7% increase from the previous year. The United States remains the world's largest market for HNWIs, followed by Japan, Germany, and China. One of the main driving forces behind this growth is the increasing number of HNWIs. The global HNWI population reached 19.6 million in 2019, a 6.3% increase from the previous year. The growth of emerging markets, particularly in Asia, has significantly contributed to this rise, with China surpassing Germany to become the third-largest market for HNWIs. Moreover, the diversification of services offered by wealth management firms has also contributed to the industry's impressive growth. Today, wealth management services go beyond traditional investment management and also include financial planning, estate planning, tax planning, and more. This shift has attracted more individuals and families to seek out wealth management services to manage their assets and secure their financial future.

Current Trends

The wealth management industry is continually evolving as market dynamics, investor needs, and technological advancements shift. One of the most notable current trends is the growing emphasis on sustainable and socially responsible investing. This means that wealth managers are not only focused on generating returns for their clients but also taking into account their clients' values and incorporating environmental, social, and governance (ESG) factors into their investment strategies. Another trend that is shaping the industry is the emergence of virtual wealth management. As people become more comfortable with using technology for their daily transactions, virtual wealth management has gained traction. This allows clients to access wealth management services remotely, making it more convenient and cost-effective, especially for those living in remote areas.

The rise of robo-advisors is also transforming the wealth management landscape. Robo-advisors, which use algorithms and technology to automatically manage investments, have gained popularity due to their lower fees and ease of use. This has led wealth management firms to incorporate robo-advisors into their services, offering a hybrid of both automated and human-led investing options. In conclusion, wealth management has come a long way from its humble beginnings, and the industry continues to evolve and adapt to the changing needs of clients. With the rise of emerging markets, the growing focus on sustainable and socially responsible investing, and the integration of technology, the future of wealth management is bright and promising. As we continue to see the industry's growth and transformation, it is clear that wealth management will remain a crucial aspect of managing and preserving wealth for generations to come.

Chapter 3: Wealth Management Fundamentals

Welcome back to the world of Wealth Management. In the previous chapter, we discussed the basics of Wealth Management and the industry as a whole. Now, let's delve deeper into the fundamentals of Wealth Management - the building blocks of creating, preserving and transferring wealth.

Wealth Creation

Wealth creation is often the starting point for many individuals seeking to grow their assets. However, creating wealth is not just about increasing one's income or maximizing returns on investments. It is also about establishing a strong financial foundation that will support sustainable growth. One of the primary keys to creating wealth is having a clear and defined financial plan. This plan should consider your current financial situation, goals, and risk tolerance. It should also be flexible and adaptable to changes in your life and the market. A well-structured financial plan can help you prioritize and allocate resources effectively, reducing the chances of making impulsive decisions that could jeopardize your wealth creation goals.

Another uncommon but crucial aspect of wealth creation is managing your debt. Debt is often seen as a financial burden, but it can also be a tool for creating wealth. By using debt wisely, such as taking out a low-interest loan to invest in a promising opportunity, you can potentially see a higher return on your investment. However, managing debt also means ensuring that your income can comfortably cover your debt payments, and staying in control of your debt load.

Lastly, diversification is critical in wealth creation. Putting all your eggs in one basket may yield substantial returns, but it also presents significant risks. By spreading your investments across different industries, asset classes, and geographic regions, you can minimize your exposure to market volatility and still see positive returns in the long run.

Wealth Preservation

As the saying goes, "it's not about how much you make, but how much you keep." This couldn't be more true when it comes to wealth preservation. After creating wealth, the next step is to protect and maintain it.

One of the main challenges in wealth preservation is inflation. As the cost of living increases, the value of your money decreases. Therefore, it is essential to invest in assets that can keep up with or outpace inflation, such as stocks, real estate, or commodities. However, it is equally important to balance these higher risk investments with stable and reliable income sources, such as bonds, annuities, and certificates of deposit.

Tax planning is another critical aspect of wealth preservation. As your wealth grows, so does your tax liability. Therefore, it is crucial to work with a financial advisor or tax specialist to implement tax-efficient strategies that can reduce your tax burden and maximize your after-tax returns. Another uncommon but significant factor in wealth preservation is insurance. Having adequate insurance coverage, such as life, health, and disability insurance, can protect your assets and loved ones in case of unforeseen circumstances. It can also prevent you from having to dip into your investments or savings to cover unexpected expenses.

Wealth Transfer

When it comes to transferring your wealth to the next generation, it is never too early to start planning. Wealth transfer involves passing down your assets to your beneficiaries while minimizing tax implications and ensuring that your wishes are carried out. Like wealth creation and preservation, wealth transfer also requires careful planning and consideration. One essential aspect of wealth transfer is estate planning. A well-crafted estate plan can help you minimize taxes, avoid probate, and ensure that your assets are distributed according to your wishes. It may also include elements such as trusts, wills, and power of attorney documents.

It is also crucial to communicate your plans and intentions to your beneficiaries. This can prevent misunderstandings and conflicts down the line and ensure that your final wishes are carried out smoothly. It is also an opportunity to educate your loved ones on financial responsibility and the proper management of their inheritance.
Lastly, regularly reviewing and updating your wealth transfer plan is crucial. As your

financial situation and goals evolve, so should your plan. A regular review can also help ensure that your plan aligns with changing tax laws and regulations.

So, there you have it - the fundamentals of Wealth Management. Wealth creation, preservation, and transfer are all interlinked and require careful consideration and planning. By understanding and implementing these fundamentals, you can set yourself on the right path to achieving your financial goals and building a sustainable legacy for future generations.

Chapter 4: Investment Strategies

Traditional vs Alternative

When it comes to investing, there are various strategies one can choose from. A common debate among investors is whether they should follow traditional or alternative investment strategies. Traditional investments include stocks, bonds, mutual funds, and real estate, while alternative investments refer to assets that are not as easily accessible, including private equity, hedge funds, and precious metals. While traditional investments have been popular for a long time, alternative investments have been gaining traction in recent years. This is due to the benefits they offer, such as diversification and potential for higher returns. However, it is important to note that alternative investments also come with higher risks and lack of liquidity compared to traditional investments. One unique alternative investment strategy is investing in art. This is an uncommon tactic in wealth management, but it offers potential for high returns and the added benefit of owning a beautiful piece of art. It also allows for investing in a passion, which can make the investment more enjoyable.

Active vs Passive

Another strategy to consider when investing is whether to take an active or passive approach. Active investing involves buying and selling investments based on market trends and trying to outperform the market, while passive investing involves buying and holding for the long term, with the goal of matching the market's performance. Proponents of the active approach argue that it allows for taking advantage of market opportunities and adapting to changing economic conditions. However, this strategy requires constant monitoring and can result in higher fees and taxes. On the other hand, passive investing offers a more hands-off approach and is typically associated with lower fees. It also allows for a more diversified portfolio and can offer lower risk compared to active investing. However, it may not provide as much potential for outperforming the market. One interesting investment strategy that combines elements of both active and passive investing is called "quant investing." This strategy uses computer algorithms to make investment decisions based on market data. It allows for a more systematic approach to investing and has shown potential for higher returns while still keeping fees low.

Growth vs Income

When it comes to investment strategies, another consideration is whether to focus on growth or income. Growth investments aim to increase in value over time, while income investments focus on generating a steady stream of income. Typically, growth investments are associated with higher risk since the focus is on potential capital appreciation. On the other hand, income investments are often considered lower risk, as they provide a source of steady income. An interesting investment strategy that combines both growth and income is known as "growth and income" investing. This approach involves investing in a mix of stocks and bonds, with the goal of achieving capital appreciation and generating income from dividends and interest. It allows for a balance between risk and stability and is suitable for investors who want to see both growth and income from their investments. In conclusion, there is no definitive answer to which investment strategy is the best. It ultimately depends on an individual's goals, risk tolerance, and preferences. Understanding the differences between traditional and alternative investments, active and passive investing, and growth and income strategies can help investors make more informed decisions and build a well-rounded portfolio. As a CWM, it is crucial to carefully consider all these options and tailor a strategy that best suits each individual client's needs.

Chapter 5: Risk Assessment: Finding a Wealthy Balance

When it comes to wealth management, assessing risk is a crucial step in developing successful investment strategies. Understanding the different types of risks, your risk tolerance, and implementing a diversified approach can lead to a healthier and more stable financial portfolio. Let's delve deeper into these topics to find the perfect balance for your wealth management journey.

Types of Risks

Before we dive into risk assessment, it's essential to understand and identify the various types of risks that can affect your investments. The most common risks in wealth management include volatility risk, inflation risk, credit risk, and market risk. Volatility risk refers to the fluctuations in the value of an investment. Some investments carry higher volatility risks than others, and it's essential to understand your risk tolerance before investing in them. Inflation risk, on the other hand, is the risk that the value of your investments will be eroded over time due to inflation. To combat this, it's crucial to seek investments that have a potential for high returns.

Credit risk is the risk of an issuer defaulting on a loan or bond. This type of risk applies mainly to fixed-income investments. Market risk, also known as systematic risk, is the risk of a particular market or sector performing poorly. It's important to note that market risk cannot be diversified or eliminated entirely, but it can be mitigated through diversification. It's important to have a good understanding of these risks as they can have a significant impact on your investment decisions. By being aware of these risks, you can make informed and calculated decisions with your financial advisor to manage and minimize their effects.

Risk Tolerance

As individuals, we all have a different tolerance for risk, and it's essential to understand where you stand on the risk spectrum. Your risk tolerance is determined by various factors, including your financial goals, time horizon, and personal preferences. Traditionally, there are three types of risk tolerance: conservative, moderate, and aggressive. Conservative investors prefer low-risk investments with a steady and predictable return. They place a high value on capital preservation and are not comfortable with market fluctuations. On the other hand, moderate investors are willing to take on a slightly higher risk for the potential of higher returns. They are looking for a balance between stable and moderate growth in their investments. Aggressive investors are willing to take on higher levels of risk in exchange for potentially higher returns. They are comfortable with volatility in the market and have a longer time horizon, allowing them to wait out any dips in the market. It's crucial to assess your risk tolerance with your financial advisor to ensure that your investment strategies align with your preferences and goals.

Diversification

One of the most common and effective ways to manage risk in wealth management is through diversification. It's the practice of spreading your investments across various asset classes, sectors, and even geographic regions to mitigate the potential effects of market fluctuations. By diversifying your portfolio, you are minimizing the impact of any single event on your investments. As the famous saying goes, "don't put all your eggs in one basket." The same applies to investments. By diversifying your portfolio, you are spreading out your risk and increasing your chances of achieving a healthy return. However, it's essential to understand that diversification does not guarantee a profit nor protect against losses; it does, however, help reduce the overall exposure to risk. It's essential to note that diversification goes beyond just investing in different assets. It also includes analyzing the correlation between investments, keeping in mind that diversification can only occur when investments have low or no correlation with each other. By utilizing a diversified approach, you are building a more resilient portfolio that can withstand various market conditions and potential risks.

A Word of Caution

In today's fast-paced and ever-evolving financial landscape, it's crucial to stay informed about new risks and market conditions that can arise. With advances in technology and changes in regulations, new risks can emerge, making it vital to revisit your risk assessment regularly.

It's also crucial to keep in mind that risk and returns are closely correlated. The higher the risk, the greater the potential for returns, but it also means a higher chance of losses. It's essential to strike a balance between risk and returns that align with your goals and risk tolerance.

In conclusion, risk assessment is a continuous and crucial process in wealth management. By understanding the different types of risks, your risk tolerance, and implementing a diversified approach, you can find a healthy balance that leads to long-term success. Remember to always consult with a financial advisor to develop a customized strategy that aligns with your unique financial goals and preferences.

Chapter 6: The Art of Building Wealth: Wealth Management Fundamentals for an Impactful Portfolio

Importance

When it comes to wealth management, one crucial aspect that cannot be overlooked is portfolio construction. The art of building a well-structured and balanced portfolio is what ultimately leads to long-term success and prosperity for investors. Every wealth manager understands that portfolios cannot be created based on a one-size-fits-all approach. It requires a deep understanding of the client's financial goals, risk appetite, and investment preferences. The importance of portfolio construction lies in its ability to align with the client's objectives and create a roadmap for success. A well-constructed portfolio can help weather the storms of market volatility, mitigate risks, and capitalize on growth opportunities. It provides a sense of security to clients and helps them achieve their financial aspirations.

Asset Classes

Diversification is the cornerstone of any well-constructed portfolio. It involves spreading your investments across asset classes to reduce risk and maximize returns. But this doesn't mean investing in every asset class out there. Not all assets are created equal. Understanding the various asset classes and their characteristics is essential while constructing a portfolio. Let's delve into some of the commonly used asset classes in wealth management. Equities: Equities or stocks represent ownership in a company. Investing in equities can offer long-term returns through capital appreciation and dividends. However, they are also considered to carry higher risks due to market volatility. Bonds: Bonds are debt instruments issued by governments or corporations. They offer fixed income and are generally considered less risky than equities. However, like any investment, they also carry risks, such as interest rate changes and default risk. Cash and Cash Equivalents: This category includes highly liquid assets such as money market funds, certificates of deposit, and treasury bills. They offer stability and can be used as a cushion during market downturns. Real Estate: Investing in real estate can provide a steady stream of income through rental properties or capital appreciation through property value appreciation. It offers diversification to a portfolio and can act as a hedge against inflation. Alternative Investments: These are investments outside the traditional asset classes, such as private equity, hedge funds, commodities, and art. They offer diversification and can potentially generate higher returns, but they also carry higher risks.

Portfolio Construction

While there is no one-size-fits-all approach to portfolio construction, certain general principles can guide wealth managers to build well-structured portfolios. These include asset allocation, diversification, risk management, and strategic rebalancing. Asset Allocation: The first step in portfolio construction is determining the right mix of assets that align with the client's risk appetite and goals. This involves selecting the suitable combination of equities, bonds, cash, and alternative investments to create a diversified and balanced portfolio that can withstand market fluctuations. Diversification: As the saying goes, "don't put all your eggs in one basket." Diversification is the key to risk management and maximizing returns in a portfolio. By spreading investments across various asset classes and sectors, investors can reduce their exposure to any one asset class and mitigate risks. Risk Management: Risk and return go hand in hand. While it is vital to take calculated risks to achieve significant returns, it is equally important to manage risks and protect the portfolio from volatility. Wealth managers can use various risk management techniques, such as diversification and hedging, to create a well-balanced portfolio. Strategic Rebalancing: Markets are unpredictable, and it's natural for the portfolio's asset mix to drift away from the desired allocation over time. Strategic rebalancing involves periodic review and reallocation of assets to maintain the desired asset mix and stay aligned with the client's goals and risk tolerance.

The Uncommon in Portfolio Construction

While the principles mentioned above may seem like the obvious approach to portfolio construction, there are some unconventional strategies that can also add value to a portfolio. These include:

Tax-Efficient Investing: Tax burden can significantly affect the returns of a portfolio. Wealth managers can implement tax-efficient strategies, such as investing in tax-free municipal bonds or utilizing tax-deferred retirement accounts, to minimize the tax impact on a portfolio. Environmental, Social, and Governance (ESG)

Investing: Investors are now increasingly concerned about making a positive impact on the world. ESG investing involves considering environmental, social, and governance factors while selecting investments. This can not only align with the clients' values but also potentially generate good returns. Impact Investing: Impact investing goes beyond ESG investing. It involves selecting investments that generate positive social and environmental impact while also aiming for financial returns. This approach can be an excellent fit for clients with a strong desire to make a difference in the world.

In Conclusion

Portfolio construction is a crucial aspect of wealth management that requires skill, knowledge, and understanding of the client's goals and preferences. A well-constructed portfolio can provide long-term growth, mitigate risks, and help clients achieve their financial goals. Wealth managers must continuously review and adapt portfolios to changing market conditions and clients' needs to ensure long-term success.

Chapter 7: Investment Strategies: Uncovering the Uncommon Factors

Company Analysis

When it comes to investment strategies, company analysis is a crucial component. Traditional company analysis typically involves examining financial statements, management structure, and competitive advantages. However, in today's ever-evolving market, there are unconventional factors that can greatly impact a company's success or failure.

For example, looking into a company's corporate culture and employee satisfaction level can give valuable insights into its potential for growth and success. Happy and driven employees often lead to better performance and innovation. Similarly, a company's social and environmental impact can directly affect its reputation and brand value. These are essential considerations that often get overlooked but can have a significant impact on investment decisions.

Furthermore, analyzing a company's response to crises or current events can provide valuable insight into its resilience and adaptability. It is rare for a company to sail through its lifespan without facing any challenges. How a company handles a crisis can be a determining factor in its long-term success. Therefore, it is necessary to look beyond the numbers and delve into the company's culture, impact, and ability to overcome obstacles.

Industry Analysis

Investment strategies should not only focus on the individual company level but also consider the broader industry landscape. Understanding the industry's current state and potential future developments is crucial in making informed investment decisions. A common practice in industry analysis is to look at market trends, competition, and supply and demand. However, going beyond the norm and looking at emerging disruptors and key players can be incredibly insightful. For example, looking into the impact of technology advancements in different industries can provide valuable information about potential future growth or decline.

Additionally, keeping an eye on regulatory changes and government policies that affect the industry can give an edge when it comes to investment decisions. For instance, changes in trade policies or environmental regulations can significantly impact certain industries, and having a thorough understanding of these factors can help adjust investment strategies accordingly.

Macroeconomic Analysis

The macroeconomic climate plays a vital role in investment strategies. While it may seem like an obvious factor to consider, investors sometimes overlook certain aspects that can greatly impact their investments. It is essential to look beyond the general economic trends and dig deeper into factors such as inflation, interest rates, and unemployment rates. A strong understanding of these elements can help predict future market movements and identify potential risks.

Moreover, global economic factors such as currency exchange rates and economic stability of key trading partners can significantly impact investments. For instance, sudden changes in political stability in a country can lead to currency devaluation, affecting multinational companies' profitability and investors' portfolios. Looking at the bigger picture and considering global macroeconomic factors can help identify risks and opportunities that may not be evident when only focusing on a specific company or industry.

Uncovering the Uncommon Factors

When it comes to investment strategies, it is crucial to look beyond the traditional metrics and considerations. Uncovering uncommon factors can provide valuable insights into a company's potential for success or failure. Some other uncommon factors to consider may include a company's customer satisfaction level, employee turnover rate, or even its CEO's public image.

Moreover, it is essential to keep an open mind and not shy away from unconventional industries or companies. The popular industries and companies may often seem like the safest and most profitable options, but exploring new territories can lead to unexpected opportunities. By analyzing companies, industries, and the macroeconomic landscape, investors can paint a comprehensive picture of the potential risks and rewards of their investment decisions. When it comes to investing, knowledge is power, and delving into unconventional factors can give investors a significant advantage.

Chapter 8: Fundamental Analysis: Charting, Indicators, and Patterns

When it comes to analyzing and understanding the financial markets, there are various methods and tools that can be used. One of the most common and widely used is fundamental analysis. This method involves examining the fundamental factors that affect the value of an asset, such as economic indicators, financial statements, and market trends. In this chapter, we will focus on charting, indicators, and patterns, which are essential tools in conducting fundamental analysis. We will explore how these elements can be used to identify potential investment opportunities and make informed decisions.

Charting

Charting, also known as technical analysis, is the process of studying past price and volume data to forecast future movements and trends. It involves the use of charts and graphs to visualize market data and identify patterns and trends that may indicate potential buying or selling opportunities. While some consider technical analysis to be more of an art than a science, it is an essential tool in the toolbox of any Chartered Wealth Manager. One of the key benefits of charting is its ability to identify support and resistance levels. Support levels are price points where buyers tend to enter the market and push prices up, while resistance levels are areas where sellers dominate and push prices down. These levels can be identified by looking at the historical price movements of an asset and plotting them on a chart. By understanding these levels, investors can make more informed decisions about when to buy or sell an asset. Another significant aspect of charting is the use of trendlines, which are lines drawn on a chart connecting the highs or lows of an asset's price movements. A trendline can help identify the direction of a trend and potential buying or selling opportunities. However, it is crucial to note that trend lines are subjective and can vary based on the time frame and chosen data points. Therefore, it is essential to use multiple trendlines to confirm the validity of a trend.

Indicators

Indicators are mathematical calculations applied to market data to provide additional insights into market trends and potential opportunities. They are used in combination with charting to confirm or contradict signals and provide a more comprehensive picture of the market. There are various types of indicators used in fundamental analysis, including trend-following indicators, oscillators, and sentiment indicators. Trend-following indicators, as the name suggests, are used to identify market trends and their strength. Popular trend-following indicators include moving averages, which smooth out price data to indicate the general direction of an asset's price, and the Relative Strength Index (RSI), which compares the magnitude of recent gains to losses to determine if an asset is overbought or oversold. Oscillators, on the other hand, are used to identify potential market reversals and overbought or oversold conditions. Examples of oscillators include the stochastic oscillator, which measures the momentum of price movements, and the MACD (Moving Average Convergence Divergence), which compares two moving averages to identify shifts in market sentiment. Sentiment indicators, such as the VIX (Volatility Index) or the put-call ratio, provide insights into market sentiment and investor behavior. These indicators can be helpful in identifying potential market turning points and when investors may be overly optimistic or pessimistic.

Patterns

Patterns, also known as chart patterns, are specific formations that occur in market data that have been proven to precede a particular market movement. Understanding and recognizing these patterns can provide investors with an edge in identifying potential opportunities and making strategic investment decisions. There are various types of patterns, with some of the most commonly used being support and resistance levels, head and shoulders, and double tops or bottoms. Each of these patterns signifies a potential shift in market sentiment and can serve as a signal for investors to take action. It is essential to note that while chart patterns are valuable in identifying potential market movements, they are not foolproof and should always be used in conjunction with other forms of analysis. Moreover, patterns tend to be more reliable in more extended time frames, such as weekly or monthly charts, rather than intraday or daily charts.

A Holistic Approach

While charting, indicators, and patterns are important tools in fundamental analysis, it is crucial to consider them in the broader context of market trends and economic factors. A holistic approach that incorporates both fundamental and technical analysis can provide a more comprehensive understanding of the markets and potential investment opportunities. In conclusion, charting, indicators, and patterns are essential elements of fundamental analysis that enable Chartered Wealth Managers to make informed decisions and identify potential market opportunities. While each of these tools has its strengths and weaknesses, using them in conjunction with each other and considering broader market dynamics can give investors a competitive edge in today's financial markets.

Chapter 9: Behavioral Finance: Understanding the Impact of Psychological Biases, Decision Making and Market Sentiments

Psychological Biases: Understanding the Human Element in Wealth Management

We often like to think of ourselves as rational beings, making decisions based on logic and reasoning. However, the field of psychology has shown us time and time again that our decisions are heavily influenced by biases and emotions. In the world of wealth management, understanding these psychological biases can make all the difference in creating successful investment strategies. One common bias in the financial world is known as the "endowment effect." This is the tendency for individuals to overvalue items or assets that they already own. In terms of wealth management, this can lead to holding onto underperforming investments simply because we have an emotional attachment to them. This bias can prevent us from making rational and logical decisions about our portfolio. Another powerful influence on decision making is the fear of loss. Studies have shown that we are more motivated to avoid losses than we are to seek gains. This can lead to irrational decisions, such as selling stocks during a market dip in fear of further losses. The key to overcoming this bias is understanding the concept of risk versus reward and having a solid investment plan in place.

Decision Making: The Importance of a Systematic Approach

Now that we understand the psychological biases that can influence our decisions, how can we ensure that we are making sound choices in our wealth management? The answer lies in having a systematic approach. This means having a clear set of rules and guidelines for making investment decisions, rather than relying on gut feelings or emotions. One example of a systematic approach is the use of stop-loss orders. This ordering system allows investors to set a predetermined price at which they will sell their investment if it drops below a certain point. This helps to limit potential losses and prevents emotional decision making. Another aspect of a systematic approach is having a diversified portfolio. This means investing in a variety of assets to reduce risk and increase potential returns. This also helps to mitigate the impact of one particular asset on the overall portfolio, preventing emotional reactions to market fluctuations.

Market Sentiments: Understanding the "Herd Mentality" and its Impact on Wealth Management

When it comes to investing, we often hear the term "market sentiment." This refers to the overall feeling or attitude of investors towards the market. Understanding market sentiments is crucial in wealth management, as it can heavily influence investment decisions. One major factor in market sentiments is the "herd mentality." This is the tendency for individuals to follow the actions of a larger group, even if it goes against their personal beliefs or logical reasoning. In terms of wealth management, this could mean buying a stock simply because everyone else is, rather than considering its fundamental value. Another factor in market sentiments is the impact of media and social media. In today's digital age, information and news spread quickly and can heavily impact market sentiments. It's important for investors to filter through the noise and make decisions based on their own research and analysis, rather than succumbing to the hype or panic created by the media.

Uncommon Knowledge: Flipping the Script in Wealth Management

In the world of wealth management, it's easy to get caught up in traditional strategies and conforming to norms. However, thinking outside the box and considering unconventional ideas and methods can often lead to success. One example of uncommon knowledge is the concept of contrarian investing. This strategy involves going against the crowd and investing in assets that are undervalued or out of favor with the majority. While this approach may go against common thinking, it can often lead to higher returns in the long run. Another uncommon approach is utilizing behavioral finance tools, such as gamification and nudges, to help individuals make better financial decisions. By tapping into the power of human psychology, these tools can shape decision making and promote positive behaviors, ultimately leading to better wealth management outcomes.

Conclusion

In the world of wealth management, understanding the impacts of psychological biases, decision making, and market sentiments is essential for success. By implementing a systematic approach, being aware of and overcoming biases, and considering uncommon knowledge, we can create more effective investment strategies and achieve our financial goals. So next time you're making a decision related to your wealth, remember to think critically, stay rational, and don't be afraid to challenge the status quo.

Chapter 10: The Importance of Goal Setting, Budgeting, and Retirement Planning in Wealth Management

As a Chartered Wealth Manager, it is essential to understand that wealth management is not just about managing money, but it is also about helping clients achieve their financial goals and dreams. This chapter will delve into the critical aspects of goal setting, budgeting, and retirement planning in wealth management and their importance in helping clients attain financial success.

Goal Setting

Goal setting is often the first step in any financial planning process, and for good reason. It serves as a roadmap for both the client and their wealth manager to determine what financial success means for them. Goals can range from short-term, such as buying a new car or taking a dream vacation, to long-term, like retirement planning and leaving a legacy. By setting clear, specific, and achievable goals, clients can have a sense of direction, and wealth managers can align their strategies accordingly. In today's society, where instant gratification is prevalent, and people are constantly bombarded with advertisements for the latest and most luxurious products, goal setting helps clients have a greater focus and discipline when it comes to their finances. It also serves as a motivation for them to make sound financial decisions that align with their objectives. As a CWM, it is crucial to not only help clients set goals but also to regularly review and adjust them as needed. Life is constantly changing, and so can a client's financial situation, so it is essential to ensure that their goals are still relevant and attainable.

Budgeting

Budgeting is often viewed as a tedious and restrictive process, but in reality, it is a powerful tool in achieving financial goals. A budget is essentially a plan that details how much money a person earns, spends, and saves. It allows individuals to have a clear understanding of their financial inflows and outflows and helps them make informed decisions on where to spend and save their money. It is common for individuals to spend more than they earn, resulting in debt and financial struggles. With budgeting, clients have a better grasp on their spending habits and can identify areas where they can cut back and save more. It also allows for better planning for big-ticket purchases, such as a new home or a child's education. In wealth management, budgeting plays a crucial role in helping clients reach their financial goals. By working closely with clients to create a realistic budget, wealth managers can ensure that they have enough resources to fund their goals and live comfortably while also building a solid financial foundation for the future.

Retirement Planning

Retirement planning is often a top priority for clients, and it should be for wealth managers as well. With the increasing life expectancy and rising healthcare costs, planning for retirement has become more critical than ever. As a CWM, it is crucial to educate clients on the different retirement planning options available, such as 401(k)s, IRAs, and Roth IRAs, and help them choose the best plans that align with their goals and risk tolerance. One key aspect of retirement planning is determining how much money a client needs to save to maintain their desired lifestyle after they stop working. This involves analyzing factors such as expected retirement age, inflation rates, current and future income, and expenses. As wealth managers, it is our responsibility to regularly review and adjust retirement plans to ensure that clients are on track to achieve their retirement goals. Retirement planning also involves considering the possibility of unexpected events, such as health issues or market downturns. It is important to have a contingency plan in place to provide financial security for clients and their families in case of these situations.

Chapter 11: Tax Planning

Tax Laws

When it comes to wealth management, it is crucial to have a solid understanding of tax laws. These laws can significantly impact your investment decisions and overall financial strategies. While it may not be the most exciting topic, being knowledgeable about tax laws can save you from costly mistakes and help you maximize your returns. Tax laws vary from country to country and can be complex, making it essential to seek guidance from a professional Chartered Wealth Manager. A CWM can help you navigate the complicated tax landscape and ensure that you are making the most tax-efficient decisions for your unique situation. One significant advantage of working with a CWM is their deep understanding of tax laws and their ability to identify and utilize tax planning strategies to your advantage. With their expertise, you can ensure that your investments are not only profitable but also tax-efficient.

Tax-Efficient Investments

Proper tax planning is not just about minimizing your tax liability; it is also about maximizing your after-tax return on investments. This is where tax-efficient investments come into play. Tax-efficient investments are those that minimize the taxes paid on any gains or income earned from them. For example, dividend-paying stocks, municipal bonds, and annuities are all considered tax-efficient investments because they are taxed at a lower rate than other investments. Having a diverse portfolio of tax-efficient investments can help you maximize your after-tax returns, allowing you to keep more of your hard-earned money. A CWM can help you identify and incorporate these types of investments into your portfolio to achieve optimal results.

Taxation on Capital Gains

Capital gains refer to the profits made from selling an asset, such as stocks or real estate. When it comes to your investments, understanding how capital gains are taxed is crucial. In most countries, capital gains are taxed at a lower rate than regular income. However, this rate can vary depending on the type of asset being sold, how long it was held, and the individual's tax bracket. For example, in the United States, short-term capital gains (assets owned for less than a year) are taxed at the same rate as regular income, while long-term capital gains (assets owned for more than a year) are taxed at a lower rate. Additionally, taxpayers in higher tax brackets may face higher tax rates on their capital gains. A CWM can help you strategically plan and time the sale of your assets to minimize the tax burden on your capital gains. They can also assist you in identifying any deductions or credits that may be applicable to your situation, further reducing your tax liability.

Uncommon Strategies for Tax Planning

While most people are familiar with traditional tax planning strategies, such as contributing to retirement accounts and using tax-efficient investments, there are some lesser-known strategies that a CWM may suggest to their clients. One such strategy is tax-loss harvesting, where an investor purposely sells losing investments to offset any capital gains and reduce their tax liability. Another option is investing in real estate investment trusts (REITs), which offer significant tax advantages for investors. There are also opportunities for tax planning through charitable giving, where individuals can receive tax deductions for their donations. A CWM can help you identify and implement these uncommon strategies to optimize your tax planning.

The Role of a CWM in Tax Planning

Tax planning is a crucial aspect of wealth management, and a CWM plays a vital role in helping individuals navigate the complex tax laws and make strategic tax planning decisions. Not only can a CWM provide expert advice on tax laws and regulations, but they can also help individuals establish long-term tax strategies that align with their financial goals. By continuously monitoring tax laws and identifying opportunities for tax planning, a CWM can ensure that their clients are making the most tax-efficient decisions for their wealth management. In conclusion, tax planning is an integral part of wealth management and should not be overlooked. By working with a qualified CWM, individuals can take advantage of tax-efficient investments and strategies, ultimately leading to greater financial success. So, whether you are a high net worth individual or a business owner, it is essential to have a solid understanding of tax laws and seek guidance from a CWM to make the most of your investments and minimize your tax liability.

Chapter 12: Wealth Transfer Strategies, Wills and Trusts, and Inheritance Tax

Wealth management is more than just building and growing a person's wealth, it also involves the transfer of that wealth to future generations. As a CWM, it is crucial to understand the various strategies and tools for wealth transfer in order to provide the best possible advice for clients. In this chapter, we will delve into the world of wealth transfer strategies, wills and trusts, and inheritance tax.

Wealth Transfer Strategies

Planning for the Future Wealth transfer strategies are all about planning for the future. It involves deciding what happens to a person's assets and wealth after they pass away. The purpose of these strategies is not just to transfer wealth to beneficiaries, but also to ensure that the transfer is done in a tax-efficient manner. One common strategy used in wealth transfer is gifting. This involves giving assets to heirs during the person's lifetime, usually in the form of cash, property, or securities. Gifting can have various benefits, such as reducing the size of the estate for inheritance tax purposes or allowing the person to see their loved ones enjoy the gifts while they are still alive. Another important strategy is estate planning, which involves creating a plan for the distribution of assets after death. This often involves the use of wills and trusts, which we will discuss in more detail below.

Wills and Trusts

Choosing the Right Tools Wills and trusts are two of the most commonly used tools in estate planning. A will is a legal document that outlines the wishes of the person after their death regarding the distribution of their assets. It also names an executor who will carry out those wishes. Trusts, on the other hand, are legal structures that are created to hold assets for the benefit of beneficiaries. They can be created during the person's lifetime (living trusts) or upon their death (testamentary trusts). Trusts can have various purposes, such as minimizing taxes, protecting assets from creditors, and providing for loved ones with special needs. When it comes to choosing between a will and a trust, it is important to consider the person's unique circumstances and goals. A will is generally less expensive and easier to set up, but it is subject to probate, which can be a lengthy and costly process. Trusts, on the other hand, can be more complex and expensive to establish, but they offer more control and privacy over the distribution of assets. Inheritance

Tax

Minimizing the Financial Burden Inheritance tax, also known as estate tax or death tax, is a tax that is imposed on the transfer of assets from a deceased person to their beneficiaries. In some countries, this tax can be quite high, and it is important to consider ways to minimize the financial burden on heirs. One common strategy used to reduce inheritance tax is through the use of trusts. By transferring assets to a trust, they are no longer considered part of the person's estate, therefore reducing the amount subject to tax. Another effective strategy is through charitable giving. By donating assets to a charity, not only is the person supporting a cause they care about, but it also reduces the value of their estate for inheritance tax purposes.

Uncommon Strategies

From Artwork to DNA Apart from the more traditional strategies, there are some more uncommon ways to transfer wealth that can be beneficial for certain individuals. One interesting strategy is the use of life insurance. By taking out a life insurance policy, the person can ensure that their beneficiaries receive a lump sum payment upon their death. This can be particularly useful for those with large estates, as it can help cover the costs of inheritance tax. Another out-of-the-box strategy is the use of artwork. Unique and valuable pieces of art can be passed down to heirs through a will without being subjected to inheritance tax. However, it is important to ensure that the artwork is properly appraised and set up to be transferred in a tax-efficient manner. In today's world, technology has also opened up new possibilities for wealth transfer. Some people are choosing to store their digital assets, such as cryptocurrency or online accounts, in trusts for future generations. There are even companies that offer DNA storage as a means of preserving a person's genetic material and passing it down to future generations. As a CWM, it is important to stay up-to-date with these uncommon strategies and be able to advise clients on the best options for their unique situations.

In closing, wealth transfer strategies, wills and trusts, and inheritance tax are all important aspects of wealth management. By understanding the various tools and strategies available, a CWM can help their clients create a solid plan for the future and ensure the smooth transfer of wealth to their loved ones. Keep in mind, every situation is different and it is essential to work closely with legal and tax professionals to determine the best solutions for each individual.

Chapter 13: Insurance Planning

Types of Insurance

Insurance is an essential aspect of wealth management, as it helps individuals and businesses protect their assets and mitigate risk. There are various types of insurance available, each serving a specific purpose. One common type of insurance is life insurance, which provides financial protection for loved ones in the event of an individual's death. There is also disability insurance and long-term care insurance, which can provide financial support if an individual becomes disabled or requires long-term care. These types of insurance are crucial for individuals as they provide a safety net in case of unforeseen circumstances. For businesses, there are various types of insurance, such as property and casualty insurance, liability insurance, and key person insurance. Property and casualty insurance protect businesses from damage to their property or equipment, while liability insurance covers legal costs and damages in case of a lawsuit. Key person insurance, on the other hand, provides financial support in case a key employee or owner becomes disabled or passes away. In addition to these common types of insurance, there are also more specialized forms, such as cyber insurance, which protects businesses from cyber attacks and data breaches, and even pet insurance, which covers vet bills for pets. As the world and economy continue to evolve, new types of insurance are also emerging, making it essential to stay updated on the options available.

Importance in Wealth Management

Insurance plays a crucial role in wealth management as it helps individuals and businesses protect their assets and financial well-being. It serves as a safety net in case of unexpected events and helps mitigate risk. For individuals, insurance can help protect their loved ones from financial hardship in case of their passing or disability. It also provides peace of mind, knowing that there are financial protections in place for themselves and their families. In wealth management, insurance is an integral part of the financial planning process. A comprehensive wealth management plan takes into account all aspects of an individual's financial situation, including potential risks and ways to mitigate them. Insurance can also play a role in tax planning, as some types of insurance may offer tax benefits. For businesses, insurance is crucial in protecting their assets and operations. It can help mitigate financial losses in case of lawsuits, damage to property or equipment, or unforeseen events. Insurance also reassures investors and stakeholders that the business has a plan in place to manage risks and protect their assets.

Risk Mitigation

One of the main reasons insurance is essential in wealth management is its role in mitigating risk. Wealth management advisors work closely with their clients to identify potential risks and develop plans to mitigate them. Insurance is one tool in that risk mitigation strategy. For example, an individual with a high net worth may have significant assets that need protection. They may invest in insurance policies such as umbrella insurance, which provides additional liability coverage above and beyond their primary insurance policies. This type of insurance can protect their assets in case of lawsuits or other unforeseen events. In case of a business, insurance is crucial in mitigating various risks. For instance, key person insurance can help protect a business in case a key employee becomes disabled or passes away. This type of insurance can provide resources to find and train a replacement and continue the company's operations. Insurance can also help businesses manage financial losses in case of property damage or legal liabilities. Insurance planning should be an ongoing process in wealth management. As individuals and businesses continue to grow and evolve, their insurance needs may change. Regular reviews and updates to insurance policies are crucial in ensuring that individuals' and businesses' assets are adequately protected. In conclusion, insurance is an essential aspect of wealth management as it offers individuals and businesses financial protection and mitigates risk. It is crucial to understand the types of insurance available and regularly review and update insurance policies to ensure they align with an individual's or business's current needs. By including insurance planning in wealth management, individuals and businesses can protect their assets and financial well-being in the face of unforeseen events.

Chapter 14: Wealth Management for High Net Worth Individuals

Unique Challenges

As a Chartered Wealth Manager (CWM), one of the most exciting and fulfilling aspects of your job will be working with high net worth individuals (HNWIs). These individuals have a unique set of challenges and needs that require specialized expertise and personalized attention. HNWIs have a high level of wealth and are typically looking for ways to preserve and grow their assets, while also planning for the future and protecting their wealth for future generations. With this level of wealth comes a unique set of challenges that require innovative solutions and a deep understanding of financial markets and risk management. One of the major challenges for HNWIs is managing their interconnected and often complex financial portfolios. They may have investments in various asset classes, such as stocks, bonds, real estate, and private equity, which need to be carefully balanced and monitored to ensure a healthy return on investment. In addition, HNWIs often have multiple sources of income, such as business ownership and investments, which require strategic planning to optimize tax efficiency and financial growth. Another challenge for HNWIs is managing their wealth beyond their lifetime. Multigenerational wealth transfer is a crucial aspect of wealth management for HNWIs, and it requires a comprehensive understanding of estate planning, tax planning, and charitable giving. As a CWM, you will have the opportunity to help HNWIs create a succession plan that aligns with their personal values and ensures the smooth transfer of wealth to future generations.

Services Offered

As a CWM, you will have access to a wide range of services to support your work with HNWIs. These services may include financial planning, tax planning, and estate planning, as well as investment management and portfolio monitoring. Additionally, you may offer specialized services, such as family office management, which involves coordinating and managing the various aspects of an HNWI's financial portfolio. This can include everything from day-to-day financial operations to estate planning and succession planning. In addition to financial and investment-related services, HNWIs may also require guidance on lifestyle and legacy planning. Wealth management for

HNWIs goes beyond just preserving and growing their financial assets – it also involves strategic planning for their lifestyle and legacy. This can include everything from philanthropy and charitable giving to lifestyle management and preserving family legacies. As a CWM, you will have the opportunity to offer guidance and expertise in these areas, helping HNWIs achieve their personal and financial goals.

International Wealth Management

With the increasing globalization of the world economy, international wealth management has become an essential aspect of wealth management for HNWIs. These individuals often have assets and investments in various countries and jurisdictions, and they require expert guidance to navigate complex international tax and wealth management strategies. As a CWM, you will need to have a deep understanding of global financial markets and regulations to effectively manage the international wealth of HNWIs. You may also need to work closely with other professionals, such as tax advisors and estate planners, to develop comprehensive and compliant strategies for managing international wealth. This aspect of wealth management for HNWIs adds a cultural and global component to your work, making it both challenging and rewarding. In conclusion, wealth management for high net worth individuals offers unique challenges and opportunities for a CWM. You will have the opportunity to work closely with individuals who have achieved significant financial success, and use your expertise and creativity to help them preserve and grow their wealth for generations to come. With a wide range of services and a global perspective, this aspect of wealth management is sure to keep you engaged and fulfilled in your career as a CWM.

Chapter 15: Wealth Management for Business Owners

As a Chartered Wealth Manager, it is important to have a thorough understanding of the complexities involved in managing the wealth of business owners. From business succession planning to employee benefits, there are many unique considerations that come into play when it comes to managing the financial well-being of a business owner. In this chapter, we will delve into the various aspects of wealth management for business owners, and uncover some uncommon insights that can help us better serve our clients.

Business Succession Planning

One of the top concerns for business owners is ensuring a successful succession plan for their business. This involves carefully planning for the transfer of ownership and management of the business to the next generation or a new owner. It is not only a financial decision, but also an emotional one as the business may have been a major part of the owner's life for many years. As a CWM, it is important to educate our clients on the various options available for business succession planning. From selling the business outright to a third party to gradually transferring ownership to family members, there are many factors to consider when making this decision. It is crucial to involve a team of experts, such as lawyers and tax advisors, to ensure a smooth and successful transition. One key factor that is often overlooked in business succession planning is the owner's personal wealth and how it will be impacted by the sale or transfer of the business. This is where a CWM can add value by providing holistic financial planning and ensuring that all aspects of the owner's wealth are taken into consideration.

Business Valuation

Business owners often have a significant portion of their wealth tied up in their business. Therefore, it is crucial to have a thorough understanding of the value of the business in order to make informed decisions about its future. Business valuation is a complex process that takes into account various factors such as the company's assets, market trends, and competition. As a CWM, it is important to have a good understanding of business valuation and be able to advise our clients on the best approach to determine the value of their business. This can involve using various methods such as discounted cash flow analysis, market multiples, or asset-based valuation. It is important to note that each method has its own limitations and it is crucial to consider all factors before arriving at a final valuation. Additionally, we must also consider the potential impact of business valuation on the owner's overall wealth and financial goals. For example, a higher valuation may result in a larger tax bill, while a lower valuation may not provide enough funds for retirement. Therefore, it is crucial to have a holistic view of the owner's financial situation and goals to make the best decisions for their business.

Employee Benefits

One of the key ways that business owners can attract and retain top talent is by offering attractive employee benefits. As a CWM, it is important to work closely with business owners to design and implement a comprehensive employee benefits package that meets the needs of their employees while considering the financial impact on the business. Uncommonly, we may come across business owners who overlook the importance of employee benefits or make decisions solely based on cost. This can result in a high turnover rate and ultimately negatively impact the business's bottom line. Therefore, it is important for us as CWMs to educate our clients on the value of offering attractive employee benefits and help them make informed decisions when designing their benefits package. In addition to traditional benefits such as health insurance and retirement plans, we can also explore unique options that may be more appealing to specific industries or employee demographics. For example, a tech company may offer stock options to their employees, while a family-owned business may provide flexible work arrangements. It is important to stay updated on the latest trends and options in employee benefits to provide the best solutions for our clients.

In Conclusion

Wealth management for business owners is not a one-size-fits-all approach. Each client will have their own unique goals, challenges, and needs that must be carefully considered in order to provide the best advice and solutions. As CWMs, it is our duty to be well-informed and continuously educate ourselves on the ever-evolving landscape of wealth management for business owners in order to provide the highest level of service to our clients. By understanding the nuances of business succession planning, business valuation, and employee benefits, we can help our clients achieve their financial goals and secure a prosperous future for their business and personal wealth.

Chapter 16: Wealth Management for Different Life Stages

Young Professionals

As a young professional, you may feel like you have your entire life ahead of you and investing may not be a top priority. However, this is the perfect time to start building a strong foundation for your future wealth. The power of compound interest means that even small investments made now can grow significantly over time. It's important to understand your risk tolerance and invest in a diversified portfolio that aligns with your long-term goals. But investing is not the only aspect of wealth management for young professionals. This is also a crucial time to establish good financial habits, such as budgeting and saving. It may seem mundane, but these habits can have a huge impact on your financial future. As a CWM, we can assist you in creating a comprehensive financial plan that includes not only investment strategies but also budgeting and goal setting. One tip for young professionals is to take advantage of employer-sponsored retirement plans, such as 401(k)s or RRSPs (Registered Retirement Savings Plans). Not only do these plans offer tax benefits, but some employers also offer matching contributions, essentially giving you free money towards your retirement savings. It's important to take advantage of these opportunities while you can.

Married Couples

For married couples, wealth management takes on a shared importance as both individuals' financial futures are intertwined. It's important for couples to have open and honest communication about their financial goals and priorities. This can prevent conflicts and ensure that both individuals are working towards the same objectives. Another aspect to consider is how to manage joint finances. Should you have joint accounts, separate accounts, or a combination of both? The decision will depend on your individual financial situation and preferences. As a CWM, we can assist you and your spouse in navigating these decisions and creating a personalized wealth management plan that suits both of your needs. Additionally, for married couples, estate planning becomes crucial. This involves creating a plan for the distribution of your assets in the event of your passing, as well as minimizing taxes and ensuring your wishes are carried out. Without proper estate planning, your loved ones may face a complicated and expensive legal process. As a CWM, we can help you create a thorough estate plan that gives you peace of mind and protects your family's financial well-being.

Retirees

Retirement doesn't mean the end of wealth management. In fact, as you enter this stage of life, it becomes even more important to actively manage your wealth to ensure a comfortable and secure retirement. The transition from accumulating wealth to drawing from it can be a daunting task, but with proper planning, it can also be a time of financial freedom. One important aspect of wealth management for retirees is managing investment risk. As you no longer have a regular income, it's important to have a well-diversified portfolio that can withstand market fluctuations. At this stage, a CWM's expertise in risk management and asset allocation can be incredibly beneficial. Also, making the most of your retirement benefits, such as Social Security or pension plans, is crucial. With proper planning, you can maximize your benefits and create a stable income stream for your retirement years. As a CWM, we can assist you in navigating the complexities of retirement benefits and help you make the most out of your hard-earned money. But retirement is not just about managing finances. It's also about enjoying the fruits of your labor and living a fulfilling life. As a CWM, we can help you create a lifestyle plan that involves not only managing your wealth but also pursuing your passions and making the most out of your retirement years. In conclusion, wealth management looks different for individuals at different life stages.

As a CWM, we understand that each person's financial situation is unique and requires a personalized approach. Our goal is to help you achieve your financial goals and dreams, regardless of your current life stage. By working together, we can create a comprehensive wealth management plan that takes into account not only your investments but also your budgeting, estate planning, and lifestyle goals. Let's embark on this journey together and build a secure and prosperous future for you and your loved ones.

Chapter 17: Client Management and Communication Strategies

Client Onboarding: Making a Memorable First Impression

In the world of wealth management, first impressions matter. Client onboarding is not just about collecting necessary documents and information. It is about making a lasting impression on your potential clients. This is the perfect opportunity to showcase your professionalism, expertise, and attention to detail, leaving a positive and lasting impression on your clients. One of the best ways to make a memorable first impression is through customization. Every client is unique and has different needs and goals. As a CWM, you have access to a wide range of resources and tools to personalize your services for your clients. This could include customized investment strategies, tailored financial plans, and personalized communication. Another crucial aspect of client onboarding is setting expectations. Be transparent with your clients about your services, fees, and timeline. This not only helps manage their expectations but also builds trust and credibility. Remember, communication is key in the onboarding process. Stay in touch with your clients regularly, provide updates on the progress, and address any concerns or questions they may have. Lastly, don't underestimate the power of small gestures. A hand-written note or a small gift can go a long way in making your clients feel valued and appreciated. These little touches can leave a lasting impression, and your clients will remember you for it.

Client Retention: Going Above and Beyond to Keep Your Clients

Retaining clients is just as crucial as acquiring new ones. Building strong and lasting relationships with your clients is the key to retention. As a CWM, you have the opportunity to not only manage your clients' wealth but also be a trusted advisor and friend. Going above and beyond for your clients will not only strengthen your relationship but also increase their loyalty. One of the most effective ways to retain clients is by providing exceptional service. This means that you should always be available to your clients, responding to their needs in a timely and efficient manner. Be proactive in your approach, anticipate their needs, and provide valuable solutions. Your clients will appreciate your dedication and commitment, and in turn, remain loyal to you. Another effective way to retain clients is through regular communication. Keep your clients informed and educated about their portfolio, market updates, and any changes or updates in the industry. This will not only demonstrate your expertise but also keep your clients engaged and interested in their wealth management. Last but not least, regularly review and evaluate your client's financial plan. As their financial goals and needs change, so should their plan. Be proactive and make any necessary adjustments to ensure that your clients' needs are met. This will not only help retain your clients but also strengthen your credibility and trust.

Communication Strategies: Cultivating Lasting Relationships

Communication is the glue that holds any relationship together. As a CWM, you have the responsibility to communicate effectively with your clients, as it is a crucial aspect of wealth management. Effective communication not only involves speaking but also listening and understanding your clients' needs and concerns. One crucial aspect of communication is listening to your clients. Active listening allows you to understand your clients' goals, needs, and concerns. By listening attentively, you can gather valuable information and tailor your services to meet your clients' needs effectively. Effective communication also involves being transparent and honest with your clients. This means providing updates, being upfront about any risks, and managing expectations. This builds trust and credibility, which are crucial in retaining and building lasting relationships with your clients. Lastly, communication is not just about providing updates and information. It also involves educating and empowering your clients. As a CWM, you have the knowledge and expertise to help your clients make informed decisions about their wealth. By educating them, you are not only adding value to their lives but also building a solid foundation for a strong and lasting relationship. In conclusion, client management and communication play a crucial role in the world of wealth management.

By going above and beyond for your clients, being transparent and proactive in your communication, and building lasting relationships, you can not only retain your clients but also cultivate a positive and successful wealth management practice.

Chapter 18: Ethics in Wealth Management

Code of Conduct

When it comes to managing an individual's wealth, it is important to have a strong sense of ethics and adhere to a code of conduct. The Chartered Wealth Manager (CWM) designation holds professionals to a high standard of ethical behavior in order to maintain the trust and confidence of their clients. This code of conduct includes principles such as honesty, transparency, and confidentiality. As a CWM, it is essential to always act in the best interest of the client and avoid any conflicts of interest. This means always providing honest and impartial advice, even if it may not align with your own interests. Trust is the foundation of any successful relationship, and in the world of wealth management, it is even more crucial.

Fiduciary Responsibility

In addition to the code of conduct, a CWM also has a fiduciary responsibility to their clients. This means that they are legally obligated to act in the best interests of their clients and manage their wealth with care, prudence, and skill. This responsibility also includes being transparent about any potential conflicts of interest and disclosing all fees and compensation to clients. Having a fiduciary responsibility means that a CWM must always put their clients' needs before their own. They cannot make decisions based on personal gain or benefit. This is a crucial aspect of maintaining trust and building a long-term relationship with clients.

Possible Conflicts of Interest

While a CWM strives to always act in the best interest of their clients, it is important to recognize and address any potential conflicts of interest that may arise. These conflicts can include personal relationships, financial incentives, or even just personal biases. To mitigate these conflicts of interest, the CWM must be transparent and communicate openly with their clients. Any potential conflicts should be disclosed and discussed to ensure that the client fully understands the situation. This transparency is not only important from an ethical standpoint but also for maintaining the trust and confidence of the client. It is also the responsibility of a CWM to continuously monitor their actions and decisions to ensure that they are not being influenced by any potential conflicts. This level of self-awareness and introspection is a key factor in maintaining ethical behavior in wealth management.

Uncommon Aspects of Ethics in Wealth Management

While the code of conduct and fiduciary responsibility are well-known and widely discussed aspects of ethics in wealth management, there are other lesser-known aspects that are just as crucial. One of these is the impact of technology on ethical behavior. With the rise of robo-advisors and automated investment systems, there is a risk of losing the personal connection and human touch in wealth management. It is important for CWMs to actively work towards maintaining ethical behavior, even in the face of advancing technology. Another aspect is being culturally sensitive and aware. With a globalized world, CWMs may have clients from different cultural backgrounds and must be mindful of their values and beliefs when providing financial advice. This includes understanding the impact of cultural biases and avoiding any unethical actions that may arise from them.

Conclusion

As a CWM, it is essential to uphold the highest ethical standards in wealth management. Trust, honesty, and integrity are the foundation of any successful client-advisor relationship. By adhering to a code of conduct, fulfilling fiduciary responsibilities, and being transparent about potential conflicts of interest, a CWM can build a reputation of trust and maintain the confidence of their clients. It is also important to remain vigilant and consider uncommon aspects of ethics in wealth management to continuously improve and maintain ethical behavior in this ever-changing industry. Always remember, the reputation of a CWM is built on their ethics and moral values.

Chapter 19: Financial Markets Overview

Stock Markets

Stock markets, also known as equity markets, are where publicly-traded companies sell shares of their company to investors. This allows companies to raise capital for growth and gives investors the opportunity to own a portion of the company's profits. One interesting aspect of the stock market is the concept of daily price fluctuations. These fluctuations are a result of the constant battle between buyers and sellers, with supply and demand dictating the price of a stock. It is not uncommon to see significant changes in stock prices from day to day, which can be influenced by a multitude of factors such as economic news, political events, and company earnings reports. The stock market is also a reflection of the overall health of the economy. In times of economic growth, stock prices tend to rise as companies are performing well and investors are optimistic. On the other hand, during an economic downturn, stock prices may decline as companies struggle and investors become more cautious. One lesser-known aspect of the stock market is the presence of high-frequency trading. This is the use of powerful computers and complex algorithms to execute trades at extremely high speeds. It has become a contentious issue as some argue that it gives an unfair advantage to those with access to this technology.

Bond Markets

The bond market, also known as the fixed-income market, is where debt securities are bought and sold. This includes government bonds, corporate bonds, municipal bonds, and more. Bonds are essentially loans made by investors to the bond issuer, with the promise of regular interest payments and the return of the principal amount at maturity. One interesting aspect of the bond market is the concept of bond ratings. These ratings are assigned by credit rating agencies and indicate the creditworthiness of a bond issuer. Bonds with higher ratings are considered less risky, but also offer lower interest rates, while bonds with lower ratings may offer higher returns but come with greater risk. Another unique feature of the bond market is its inverse relationship with interest rates. When interest rates go up, bond prices tend to go down, and vice versa. This is because the fixed interest payments of bonds become less attractive compared to other investments when interest rates rise. Lastly, a commonly misunderstood aspect of the bond market is the role of bond mutual funds. These funds invest in a portfolio of bonds and offer investors a way to diversify their bond holdings without having to purchase individual bonds. It's important to note that bond mutual funds are subject to market fluctuations and do not offer a guaranteed rate of return.

Foreign Exchange Markets

Foreign exchange markets, also known as forex or FX markets, are where currencies from different countries are bought and sold. This market is the largest in the world, with an average daily trading volume of over $5 trillion. One unique characteristic of the foreign exchange market is its decentralization. Unlike stock and bond markets, there is no central location where forex trades take place. Instead, it operates electronically through a network of banks, brokers, and other financial institutions. The foreign exchange market is also constantly fluctuating, with exchange rates changing by the second. Factors such as economic data, political events, and central bank policies can all have an impact on currency values. This makes it a highly liquid and volatile market, with potential for both high profits and high losses. Finally, an interesting aspect of the foreign exchange market is the concept of currency pairings. Currencies are always traded in pairs, with the exchange rate indicating how much of one currency is needed to buy a unit of another currency. Some of the most commonly traded pairs include USD/EUR, USD/JPY, and GBP/USD. As a Chartered Wealth Manager, having a thorough understanding of these important financial markets is crucial in providing sound investment advice to clients. By staying abreast of the latest market developments and trends, CWMs can make informed investment decisions and help clients achieve their financial goals.

Chapter 20: Economics in Wealth Management

When it comes to wealth management, understanding the economic environment is crucial for making informed investment decisions. Economic indicators, emerging markets, and trade agreements are all important factors to consider in this ever-changing landscape. In this chapter, we will delve deeper into the role of economics in wealth management and how it affects the strategies used by Chartered Wealth Managers.

Economic Indicators

Economic indicators provide valuable insights into the health of the economy and help to forecast future trends. As a Chartered Wealth Manager, it is important to keep a close eye on these indicators as they can have a significant impact on investment decisions. Some common economic indicators include GDP, inflation rate, interest rates, and unemployment rate. However, in addition to these mainstream indicators, there are also uncommon ones that can provide unique perspectives on the economy. For example, the Baltic Dry Index, which measures the cost of shipping raw materials, is a good indicator of global economic activity. Another uncommon indicator is the Big Mac Index, which compares the cost of buying a Big Mac in different countries and can reveal disparities in currency values.

Emerging Markets

As wealth managers, it is important to diversify investment portfolios and explore opportunities in emerging markets. Emerging markets refer to developing countries with rapidly growing economies, such as China, India, and Brazil. These markets offer a potential for high returns but also come with higher risks. One key trend to watch in emerging markets is the rise of the middle class and their purchasing power. As more individuals move up the socioeconomic ladder, there is an increased demand for luxury goods and services, creating opportunities for investors. However, it is important to thoroughly research and understand the political and economic climate of these markets before making any investment decisions.

Trade Agreements

The global economy is closely intertwined, and trade agreements play a significant role in shaping it. These agreements between countries or groups of countries aim to reduce trade barriers and promote economic cooperation. As a Chartered Wealth Manager, it is important to analyze the impact of these agreements on different industries and sectors. Besides monitoring established trade agreements, it is also important to keep an eye on emerging ones. One example is the African Continental Free Trade Agreement, which aims to create the world's largest free trade area. This agreement presents opportunities for businesses and investors to tap into the potential of the African market.

Adapting to an Ever-Changing Economic Landscape

The world of economics is ever-changing, and as a Chartered Wealth Manager, it is important to stay informed and adaptable to uncertainties and evolving trends. This requires continuous education and staying up-to-date with industry developments. Technology has also impacted the economic landscape, making it easier to access information and track economic indicators in real-time. As wealth managers, embracing technology and using it to our advantage can help us make better decisions for our clients. Moreover, staying true to the fundamentals of wealth management, such as asset allocation and risk management, can help navigate through economic uncertainties. As the saying goes, 'the best defense is a good offense.'

Incorporating Uncommon Factors in Wealth Management

While economic indicators, emerging markets, and trade agreements are crucial aspects of wealth management, it is also important to consider uncommon factors that may impact investments. These can include cultural and social trends, demographic shifts, and even changes in consumer behavior. For example, the rise in eco-consciousness has led to a shift in consumer behavior, with a growing demand for environmentally and socially responsible investments. As a Chartered Wealth Manager, considering these factors can lead to a more holistic and comprehensive approach to wealth management.

Continuing Education and Networking

To excel in wealth management and adapt to an ever-changing economic landscape, continuous education and networking are key. Attending conferences and seminars, networking with industry experts, and keeping up-to-date with the latest industry news and developments can help improve skills and expand knowledge in this constantly evolving field.

In conclusion, economics plays a vital role in wealth management, and as Chartered Wealth Managers, it is important to not only focus on mainstream indicators but also consider uncommon factors. Adapting to change, staying informed, and continuously learning are essential in providing the best service to clients and achieving success in this dynamic field.

Chapter 21: Investment Products

When it comes to building your investment portfolio, having a diverse range of investment products can help you achieve your financial goals. While there are many choices available, we will focus primarily on three key investment products in this chapter: stocks, bonds, and mutual funds. These products are commonly used by wealth managers and investors, but we will also delve into some uncommon or lesser-known features of these products.

Stocks

Most people are familiar with stocks as a form of investment, but do you know the origins of the stock market? The early history of stocks can be traced back to 12th-century France, where merchants and traders would meet to buy and sell debt obligations. This practice continued to evolve over the centuries, eventually leading to the creation of modern stock exchanges. Today, stocks are a popular investment choice due to their potential for long-term growth and the opportunity to earn dividends. However, there are also different types of stocks, such as common and preferred stocks, as well as classes of stock with different voting rights. Understanding these differences can help investors make more informed decisions about their holdings. While stocks are generally considered a high-risk investment, there are some unique ways to mitigate this risk. For example, dividend stocks, which pay regular dividends, can provide a steady stream of income regardless of market fluctuations. Additionally, using a dollar-cost averaging strategy, where you invest a fixed amount at regular intervals, can help reduce the impact of market volatility on your returns.

Bonds

Unlike stocks, which represent ownership in a company, bonds are a form of debt. Governments, corporations, and even municipalities issue bonds to raise money for various projects and operations. When an investor purchases a bond, they are essentially loaning money to the issuer, with the promise of regular interest payments and the return of the initial investment at a specified time in the future. Bonds are typically perceived as a lower-risk investment compared to stocks, but they can still carry their own set of risks. For instance, bond prices can fluctuate depending on the interest rate environment and the creditworthiness of the issuer. In some cases, investors may consider high-yield or junk bonds, which offer higher interest rates but come with a higher risk of default. One uncommon type of bond that investors may not be familiar with is catastrophe bonds. These are issued by insurance companies and are designed to transfer the risk of natural disasters, such as hurricanes or earthquakes, to investors. In the event of a catastrophe, the issuer would not have to repay the principal and interest to investors, instead using the funds to cover the costs of the disaster.

Mutual Funds

Mutual funds are a popular choice for investors who prefer a hands-off approach to managing their investments. These are professionally managed funds that pool money from multiple investors to buy a diversified portfolio of stocks, bonds, or other assets. Essentially, investors buy shares in the mutual fund, and the value of those shares is determined by the performance of the underlying assets. One of the main benefits of mutual funds is their diversification. By investing in a mutual fund, investors gain exposure to a variety of assets, reducing the risk of relying on a single stock or bond. Mutual funds also offer the potential for steady returns through regular dividend payments, and they are relatively liquid, meaning investors can buy and sell shares at any time. While mutual funds are mainly considered a long-term investment vehicle, there are also short-term mutual funds that offer potential gains in just a few months. These funds are suitable for investors who have shorter investment horizons or are looking for more immediate returns.

Chapter 21: Unusual Investment Choices

In addition to traditional stocks, bonds, and mutual funds, there are also some less commonly known investment options available. These unique instruments offer different opportunities for investors, but they also come with their own set of risks and complexities.

Real Estate Investment Trusts (REITs)

REITs are companies that own or operate income-generating real estate properties. These can include commercial buildings, apartment complexes, and shopping centers, among others. By investing in REITs, investors receive regular dividends and the potential for long-term capital appreciation. One significant advantage of REITs is that they offer a way for individuals to invest in real estate without the hassle of owning and managing physical properties. It also provides a form of diversification outside of traditional stocks and bonds.

Exchange-Traded Funds (ETFs)

ETFs are similar to mutual funds in that they hold a basket of assets. However, they differ in that they can be traded like stocks on an exchange. This means that investors can buy and sell ETFs throughout the day, whereas mutual fund trades only occur at the end of the trading day. ETFs offer investors another way to diversify their portfolios and gain exposure to different markets and sectors. They also tend to have lower fees compared to mutual funds, making them an attractive option for cost-conscious investors.

Cryptocurrencies

Cryptocurrencies, such as Bitcoin and Ethereum, have gained popularity as a form of virtual currency. While they are highly volatile and still relatively new, they offer the potential for significant gains for those with a high risk tolerance. Investing in cryptocurrencies requires a thorough understanding of the technology and market forces driving their value. It is also crucial to research the regulations in your country, as they can vary significantly from place to place. In conclusion, while stocks, bonds, and mutual funds remain essential investment products, there are also some unique and lesser-known choices available. These options offer investors different opportunities to diversify their portfolios and potentially achieve their financial goals. However, it is essential to thoroughly research and understand the risks associated with each investment product before making any decisions. As a CWM, being knowledgeable about these options and their intricacies can help you provide comprehensive and tailored investment advice to your clients.

Chapter 22: Alternative Investments

Alternative investments have gained popularity in recent years as investors seek new ways to diversify their portfolios and potentially achieve higher returns. These investments, also known as "non-traditional" or "exotic" investments, often include private equity, hedge funds, and real estate.

Private Equity

Private equity is a form of investment in which capital is invested in companies that are not publicly traded. This type of investment is usually made by private equity firms, which raise funds from investors and use them to acquire stakes in companies. Private equity firms often work closely with management teams to improve the company's performance and ultimately sell their stake for a profit. One interesting aspect of private equity is its focus on long-term investments. While traditional investments in stocks and bonds are typically held for a shorter period of time, private equity investments may be held for five years or more. This requires patience and a long-term perspective, as the success of the investment may not be seen immediately. Additionally, private equity investments often have a high barrier to entry, as they are typically only available to wealthy individuals and institutional investors. This exclusivity can make private equity an elusive and alluring investment opportunity for many.

Hedge Funds

Hedge funds are investment vehicles that pool funds from investors and use various investment strategies to generate returns. These strategies can include long and short positions, leverage, and derivatives. Hedge funds often have a higher level of risk and complexity than traditional investments, making them more suitable for sophisticated investors. One interesting aspect of hedge funds is their ability to provide alternative sources of income, as their strategies can be less correlated with traditional investments. This makes hedge funds a potential diversification tool for investors looking to mitigate risk. It's worth noting that hedge funds are notoriously secretive, with little information about their investments and performance available to the public. This air of mystery can add to their allure and attract investors who are looking for something different.

Real Estate

Real estate is a tangible form of alternative investment that involves buying and owning physical property. This can include residential, commercial, or industrial properties, as well as land and real estate investment trusts (REITs). One uncommon aspect of real estate as an investment is the potential to generate passive income. By renting out a property, investors can earn a steady stream of rental income without having to actively manage the property. Real estate investments also have the potential for appreciation in value, as properties may increase in price over time. This can provide a cushion against inflation and potentially result in a profit when the property is sold. However, like all investments, real estate also carries risks. Property values can fluctuate, and there are costs associated with maintenance and property management. Additionally, real estate investments often require a significant amount of capital, making it a less accessible alternative investment for some investors.

Conclusion

Alternative investments can offer unique opportunities for investors to diversify their portfolios and potentially achieve higher returns. Private equity, hedge funds, and real estate are just a few examples of alternative investments that can add depth and complexity to an investment portfolio. However, it's essential for investors to thoroughly understand the risks and costs associated with these types of investments before diving in. It's also crucial to have a long-term perspective and a well-diversified portfolio to mitigate risk. With careful consideration and the help of a knowledgeable advisor, alternative investments can be a valuable addition to any investor's arsenal.

Chapter 23: Financial Instruments in Wealth Management

Financial instruments play a crucial role in wealth management. They are essentially contracts that represent an ownership position in a financial asset, which can be traded in the market. These instruments offer investors the opportunity to diversify their portfolio and potentially increase their return on investment. In this chapter, we will explore the world of financial instruments, such as derivatives, options, and futures, and discuss their role in wealth management.

Derivatives

One of the most popular and widely used financial instruments in wealth management is derivatives. A derivative is a contract between two or more parties that derives its value from an underlying asset. The underlying asset could be anything from commodities, currencies, stocks, or interest rates. Derivatives come in various forms, such as options, futures, forwards, and swaps. One of the most common uses of derivatives in wealth management is for hedging purposes. Hedging is a risk management strategy that involves using derivatives to offset potential losses in a portfolio. For example, an investor could use a derivative contract to protect their portfolio from a potential decline in the stock market. This could be particularly useful for high net worth individuals who have a significant portion of their assets invested in the stock market.

Options

Options are another popular financial instrument in wealth management. An option gives the holder the right, but not the obligation, to buy or sell an underlying asset at a predetermined price within a specified period. There are two types of options: call options and put options. A call option gives the holder the right to buy an asset, while a put option gives the holder the right to sell an asset. One of the key benefits of options in wealth management is their flexibility. They can be used for various purposes, such as speculating on market movements, hedging against potential losses, or generating income through covered calls. However, options also come with significant risks and are not suitable for all investors. Proper risk management and understanding the market dynamics are crucial when using options in wealth management.

Futures

Futures are another type of financial instrument widely used in wealth management. A futures contract is an agreement between two parties to buy or sell an underlying asset at a predetermined price and date in the future. Futures are commonly used for speculative purposes, such as predicting the future price of a commodity or currency. Futures are also used for hedging purposes, similar to derivatives. For example, a business owner who relies on a particular commodity for their business operations could use futures to hedge against potential price fluctuations. Futures have become increasingly popular in the world of wealth management, as they provide investors with exposure to various asset classes, such as commodities, currencies, and stock indexes.

Uncommon Uses of Financial Instruments

While derivatives, options, and futures are widely used in wealth management, there are some lesser-known uses of financial instruments that can be quite beneficial for investors. One uncommon use is for tax planning purposes. For example, investors can use derivatives to offset capital gains and reduce their tax liability. Another uncommon use is for estate planning. Investors can use insurance-linked securities, a type of derivative, to protect their estate from potential market risks. This can be particularly useful for investors who wish to pass down their wealth to future generations. Financial instruments can also be used for philanthropy and charitable giving. By utilizing options and futures, investors can donate a portion of their portfolio gains to charitable causes without having to sell off their assets.

The Role of a Wealth Manager

Given the complexities and risks associated with financial instruments, the role of a wealth manager becomes even more critical. A wealth manager is a qualified and experienced professional who helps individuals and families manage their wealth effectively. They use their expertise and knowledge to develop investment strategies tailored to their client's goals and risk tolerance. A wealth manager's responsibilities may include asset allocation, selecting suitable investment products, monitoring performance, and providing financial advice. They also play a crucial role in managing the risks associated with financial instruments such as derivatives, options, and futures. A wealth manager's ultimate goal is to help their clients achieve their financial objectives and maintain their wealth for future generations.

Conclusion

Financial instruments such as derivatives, options, and futures are powerful tools in the world of wealth management. They offer investors opportunities to diversify their portfolio, hedge against potential market risks, and generate income. However, it is essential to understand the risks involved and seek professional advice from a wealth manager before engaging in these investments. With proper knowledge and guidance, financial instruments can play a significant role in helping individuals and families secure their financial future.

Chapter 24: Impact of Technology in Wealth Management

Technology has always played a crucial role in the financial industry, and the world of wealth management is no exception. With the rapid advancements we are seeing in various areas of technology, the impact on wealth management is becoming more prominent than ever before. In this chapter, we will explore the various ways in which technology is shaping the world of wealth management, and how it's changing the game for investors and advisors alike.

Robo-advisors

Robo-advisors have been a hot topic in the financial industry in recent years. These digital platforms use algorithms and technology to provide automated financial advice and investment management services. They have recently gained a lot of popularity due to their low fees and user-friendly interfaces. But are they really a threat to the traditional wealth management model? Well, the answer is not as simple as a yes or no. While robo-advisors do have certain advantages, they still lack the human touch and personalized advice that a traditional wealth manager can provide. Another concern is the reliance on technology, which can be prone to error and may not always be able to adapt to market changes. However, some wealth management firms are finding ways to incorporate robo-advisor technology into their existing services, creating a hybrid model that combines the best of both worlds.

Digital Banking

Digital banking has revolutionized the way we do our banking and manage our finances. It has also had a significant impact on the world of wealth management. With the rise of mobile banking and online financial tools, investors now have easy access to their accounts and investments at any time and from anywhere in the world. This has made it easier for wealth managers to monitor and manage their clients' portfolios, and for investors to stay informed and make timely investment decisions. Furthermore, digital banking has also opened up the world of wealth management to a broader audience. With the accessibility and convenience of online banking, more individuals are now able to invest and manage their wealth, rather than being limited to the wealthy elite.

Artificial Intelligence

Artificial intelligence (AI) is another game-changer in the world of wealth management. Through machine learning and data analysis, AI can quickly and accurately identify patterns and make predictions about market trends and investment opportunities. This has helped advisors and investors make more informed decisions and minimize risk. In addition, AI algorithms can also analyze an individual's financial habits and goals and provide personalized investment advice and financial planning. This level of customization was previously only available to high net worth individuals with access to top-tier wealth management services.

Unconventional Solutions

While robo-advisors, digital banking, and artificial intelligence are the more commonly discussed advancements in wealth management technology, there are other less conventional solutions that are also making waves. For example, blockchain technology is being explored as a way to increase transparency and security in financial transactions and streamline the wealth management process. Virtual reality is also emerging as a potential tool for wealth management. It can provide a fully immersive and interactive experience, allowing investors to visualize and understand their investments in a whole new way. This could potentially change the way investors make decisions and interact with their wealth managers.

The Importance of Human Touch

Despite all the advancements in technology, one cannot deny the importance of the human element in wealth management. Building and maintaining relationships with clients is a crucial aspect of wealth management, and technology can never fully replace that. Human advisors can provide empathy, emotional support, and personalized attention that technology simply cannot. Moreover, as technology continues to evolve, it is essential for wealth management professionals to adapt and embrace it. The key is to find a balance between using technology as a tool to enhance the client experience and still providing the personalized touch that is essential in wealth management. In conclusion, technology has become an integral part of wealth management, and its impact on the industry is only expected to grow in the future. While it brings about many positive changes and opportunities, it is also essential to remember that the human element should never be overlooked or replaced. By finding the right balance between technology and the human touch, wealth management professionals can continue to provide high-quality services to their clients and stay ahead in the ever-changing landscape of financial technology.

Chapter 25: Impact of Technology in Wealth Management

Technology has changed the way we do things in our daily lives, from how we communicate to how we shop. And the financial industry is no exception. Wealth management, in particular, has seen a major shift with the integration of technology in its processes. In this chapter, we will delve into the impact of technology in wealth management, specifically in the context of ESG (Environmental, Social, and Governance) criteria, impact investing, and sustainable development goals. ESG criteria refer to the standards used by companies to evaluate their performance in terms of environmental, social, and governance factors. These factors are becoming increasingly important for investors who want to align their investments with their values.

With the help of technology, wealth managers now have easier access to data on a company's ESG practices, allowing them to make more informed decisions for their clients. For instance, there are now software tools that can screen and analyze companies based on their ESG performance, providing wealth managers with a more comprehensive view of a company's sustainability efforts. Furthermore, technology has also made it easier for wealth managers to track and monitor the progress of their clients' investments in terms of ESG performance. With the use of digital platforms and analytics tools, wealth managers can provide their clients with real-time updates on how their investments are contributing to sustainable practices.

This level of transparency and accountability is crucial for clients who are looking to make a positive impact with their investments. Impact investing, on the other hand, refers to the practice of investing in companies or organizations that have the intention to generate positive social or environmental impact in addition to financial return. This type of investing is becoming increasingly popular, especially among younger generations who are more conscious about the impact of their financial decisions. With the help of technology, wealth managers can now easily screen and identify potential impact investments for their clients.

This is done through the use of algorithms and data-driven analysis, which has made the process more efficient and accurate. In fact, some wealth management firms have even developed their own impact investing platforms, allowing clients to choose from a range of impact investment options based on their personal preferences and values. This not only makes it easier for clients to invest in companies that align with their values but also creates a more personalized and engaging experience for them.

Sustainable development goals (SDGs) also play a significant role in the integration of technology in wealth management. The SDGs, adopted by the United Nations in 2015, are a set of 17 global goals that aim to end poverty, protect the planet, and ensure prosperity for all. Wealth managers can use technology to identify companies or projects that contribute to these goals and offer them as investment options to their clients. This not only helps clients make a positive impact with their investments but also supports the achievement of these global goals. Moreover, technology has also made it easier for wealth managers to educate their clients on the importance of sustainable investments and the positive impact they can make. With the use of digital platforms and social media, wealth managers can reach a wider audience and share valuable information and resources on impact investing and sustainable development goals. This not only creates awareness but also empowers clients to make more informed investment decisions. It's worth noting that technology has also brought about challenges in wealth management, particularly in terms of cybersecurity and privacy concerns.

With the increasing amount of data being shared and stored online, wealth managers need to ensure that their clients' information is secure and protected at all times. This requires the implementation of robust security measures and staying updated with the latest advancements in cybersecurity. In conclusion, technology has transformed the way wealth management operates, especially in terms of incorporating ESG criteria, impact investing, and sustainable development goals. With the help of technology, wealth managers can now provide their clients with more personalized, transparent, and sustainable investment options, making a positive impact in the financial industry. However, it is crucial for wealth managers to also address any challenges that may arise and ensure the safety and security of their clients' information. Embracing technology in wealth management can lead to a more sustainable and promising future for both the industry and the world.

Chapter 26: Investment Strategies for Retirement Planning

Retirement planning is a crucial aspect of wealth management, and as a Chartered Wealth Manager, it is important to have a thorough understanding of different investment strategies that can help clients achieve their retirement goals. In this chapter, we will discuss some common investment strategies as well as some uncommon ones that are often overlooked but can be beneficial for retirement planning.

Annuities

Annuities are often a misunderstood investment vehicle, but they can be a valuable component of a retirement plan. Annuities are essentially a contract between an insurance company and an individual, where the individual makes a lump sum payment or a series of payments, and in return, the insurance company provides a guaranteed stream of income during retirement. One of the main benefits of annuities is the guaranteed income they offer, which can provide peace of mind for retirees. Additionally, annuities have tax-deferred growth, meaning earnings are not taxed until withdrawals are made. This can be helpful for those in a higher tax bracket during their working years. However, it is important to note that withdrawals from annuities are taxed as ordinary income.

Systematic Withdrawal Plans

Systematic withdrawal plans (SWPs) are a lesser-known but effective way to generate steady income during retirement. With an SWP, investors can set up a schedule of regular withdrawals from a mutual fund or a portfolio of investments. This allows for a systematic and consistent stream of income for retirees. One of the unique aspects of SWPs is that they can offer flexibility in managing cash flow during retirement. Investors can adjust the withdrawal amount or even temporarily pause withdrawals during times of market volatility. This can help avoid the need to sell investments at a loss in order to generate income.

Long-Term Care Insurance

While it may not be a traditional investment, long-term care insurance is an important consideration for retirement planning. As people are living longer, the chances of needing some form of long-term care increase, and the costs can be significant. Long-term care insurance provides coverage for expenses related to long-term care, such as nursing homes, assisted living, and home health care. By having this coverage in place, retirees can protect their retirement assets from being depleted by unforeseen expenses. One uncommon but valuable aspect of long-term care insurance is the ability to add riders for inflation protection. This ensures that coverage keeps pace with increasing costs of care, providing a comprehensive safety net for retirees.

Uncommon Strategies

While we have discussed some common investment strategies for retirement planning, it is important to also consider uncommon strategies that can be beneficial for certain individuals. For example, for high-income earners who may be limited on traditional retirement account contributions, investing in real estate through a self-directed IRA can provide tax benefits and diversification. Another uncommon strategy is using a Health Savings Account (HSA) as a retirement investment tool. HSAs are often thought of as a way to save for current and future medical expenses, but they can also be used as a way to save for retirement. Contributions are tax-deductible, growth is tax-free, and withdrawals for qualified medical expenses are tax-free. However, after the age of 65, withdrawals can be made penalty-free for non-medical expenses, making it a valuable retirement savings vehicle. Additionally, considering alternative investments such as private equity, hedge funds, and venture capital can provide diversification and potentially higher returns for retirement portfolios. These investments are often reserved for accredited investors, but they can offer unique opportunities for high net worth individuals.

In Conclusion

As a Chartered Wealth Manager, it is important to have a comprehensive understanding of investment strategies for retirement planning. While traditional strategies such as stocks, bonds, and mutual funds are important components, it is also beneficial to explore uncommon strategies that can provide additional benefits and diversification. Annuities, systematic withdrawal plans, and long-term care insurance are just a few examples of uncommon yet valuable strategies to consider for retirement planning.

Chapter 27: Investment Strategies for Education Planning

Introduction

In this chapter, we will explore investment strategies specifically for education planning. As every parent knows, providing for your child's education can be a significant financial burden. However, with proper planning and the right investment strategies, you can secure your child's future without compromising your own financial goals. 529 Plans One of the most popular investment strategies for education planning is the 529 plan. This is a tax-advantaged savings plan specifically designed for higher education expenses. It can be used to pay for tuition, fees, room and board, and other qualified education expenses at eligible institutions. The funds in a 529 plan grow tax-free, and withdrawals are also tax-free as long as they are used for qualified education expenses. What makes 529 plans even more attractive is that they are not limited to just parents. Grandparents, aunts, uncles, and even friends can contribute to a 529 plan for a child's education. This means that the burden of saving for education doesn't have to fall solely on the parents' shoulders. One uncommon advantage of 529 plans is that they can also be used for K-12 education expenses, not just higher education. This includes private school tuition, which can be a significant financial burden for many families. So, even if your child decides not to pursue higher education, the funds in a 529 plan can still be put to good use.

Education Savings Accounts

Education Savings Accounts (ESAs) are another tax-advantaged investment vehicle for education planning. They allow individuals to contribute up to $2,000 per year, per child, until the child turns 18. The funds in an ESA can be used for both primary and secondary education expenses, including tuition, fees, and textbooks. One uncommon feature of an ESA is that the funds can be invested in a wide range of securities, including stocks, bonds, and mutual funds. This gives the owner more control over the investment and potentially higher returns than a traditional savings account. However, one limitation of ESAs is that the contributions are not tax-deductible. This means that while the funds grow tax-free, you do not receive a tax break for your contributions like you would with a 529 plan. Scholarships Investing in education doesn't always have to come from your own savings. Scholarships are an excellent way for students to receive financial support for their education without having to pay it back. As a wealth manager, part of your role will be to educate your clients on the different types of scholarships available and help them find and apply for them. While academic scholarships for high-performing students are the most well-known, many other scholarships are also available, such as athletic scholarships, merit-based scholarships, and need-based scholarships. It's essential to work with your clients to find the right scholarships for their child's unique strengths and interests to increase their chances of being awarded one. One uncommon type of scholarship that is gaining popularity is the "no-strings-attached" scholarship. These are awarded based on random draws or unusual criteria, such as being left-handed or having a specific last name. While these may be less predictable, they can be a fun and unexpected way to get financial support for education expenses.

Tips for Successful Education Planning

Now that we have explored some of the investment strategies for education planning let's look at some tips for successful education planning:

1. Start Early: The earlier you start saving for your child's education, the more time there is for your investments to grow.

2. Consider Your Risk Tolerance: Education planning is a long-term goal, which means you can take on more risk than you would with short-term investments. This can potentially result in more significant returns, but also higher levels of risk. It's crucial to find a balance between risk and reward that aligns with your risk tolerance.

3. Diversify Your Investments: As with any investment strategy, it's essential to diversify your portfolio. This means investing in a mix of different asset classes, such as stocks, bonds, and real estate.

4. Communicate with Your Child: Involve your child in the conversation and educate them about the importance of saving for their education. This will not only help them understand the value of the funds but also get them excited and motivated to work towards their educational goals.

Conclusion

Education planning is a crucial aspect of wealth management, and with the right strategies, it can be a manageable and rewarding experience for both parents and their children. By understanding the different investment options available and following the tips we have outlined, you can secure your child's future while also working towards your financial goals. As a Chartered Wealth Manager, you have the expertise and knowledge to guide your clients towards a successful education planning journey.

Chapter 28: Investment Strategies for Charitable Giving

Charitable giving is not only a way to support causes and organizations that are important to us, but it can also have significant benefits for our personal financial planning. As a Chartered Wealth Manager (CWM), it is important to not only have a deep understanding of investment strategies for wealth management, but also for charitable giving.

Donor-Advised Funds

One common way of giving to charity is through donor-advised funds (DAFs). These are charitable giving accounts that allow individuals to make a charitable contribution, receive an immediate tax deduction, and then recommend grants from the account to IRS-approved charitable organizations. DAFs are a popular choice for those who want to plan their contributions over a period of time, as the funds can be invested and potentially grow over time before being distributed to charities. One uncommon way of using a DAF is to donate appreciated assets, such as stocks or real estate, instead of cash. This can provide the donor with a larger tax deduction, potentially eliminate capital gains taxes, and still allow for them to recommend grants to charities over time. It also allows for more strategic giving, as appreciated assets can be donated to charities that are aligned with the donor's values and have a long-term impact.

Charitable Trusts

Charitable trusts are another powerful tool for charitable giving. A charitable remainder trust (CRT) allows an individual to place assets into a trust and receive an income from the trust for a specified number of years or for life. Upon the donor's death or after the specified time period, the remaining assets in the trust are donated to a charity of their choice. This not only provides income for the donor during their lifetime, but also allows for a significant charitable contribution. On the other hand, a charitable lead trust (CLT) allows the donor to transfer assets into a trust and have them distributed to a designated charity for a certain period of time. Once this time period ends, the remaining assets are passed on to beneficiaries, such as family members or other loved ones. This strategy can be useful for individuals who have assets they want to pass on to their loved ones, but also want to support a cause they care about during their lifetime.

Tax Benefits

Aside from the obvious benefits of giving to charity, such as supporting a cause and making a positive impact, there are also significant tax benefits to consider. In the United States, individuals who itemize their deductions can deduct up to 60% of their adjusted gross income for cash donations to charities, and up to 30% for donations of appreciated assets to public charities. This can result in substantial tax savings, especially for high net worth individuals. Investment strategies for charitable giving also play a role in minimizing tax liabilities. By utilizing tax-efficient investments, such as exchange-traded funds (ETFs) or municipal bonds, investors can potentially increase their charitable deductions while also reducing their overall tax burden. It is important to note, however, that there are certain restrictions and guidelines in place for charitable donations, and it is crucial to consult with a tax professional to ensure compliance and maximize tax benefits.

Uncommon Strategies

While donor-advised funds and charitable trusts are more commonly known strategies for charitable giving, there are other, less commonly used methods that may be beneficial for certain individuals. One example is giving directly from an IRA. Individuals over the age of 70 ½ who have traditional IRAs are required to take minimum distributions each year, which are subject to income taxes. However, they can choose to donate up to $100,000 from their IRA to charity and exclude it from their taxable income. This not only fulfills their required minimum distribution, but also provides significant tax benefits. Another uncommon strategy is donating life insurance policies to charity. Individuals can make a charity the beneficiary of a life insurance policy, and upon their death, the charity would receive the death benefit. This can provide a sizable contribution to a charity at a relatively low cost for the donor.

Incorporating Charitable Giving into Financial Planning

As a CWM, it is important to understand how to incorporate charitable giving into the overall financial planning of clients. By incorporating tax planning and investment strategies specific to charitable giving, you can help clients achieve their philanthropic goals while also maximizing tax benefits and minimizing tax liabilities. It is also important to stay informed about new and uncommon strategies that may benefit clients and improve their overall financial plan. In conclusion, investment strategies for charitable giving are a crucial component of wealth management. By utilizing tools such as donor-advised funds and charitable trusts, understanding tax benefits, and staying informed about uncommon strategies, CWMs can help clients achieve their philanthropic goals while also enhancing their financial planning. As a CWM, it is important to not only understand these strategies, but also to actively incorporate them into clients' financial plans to help them achieve their objectives and make a positive impact in the world.

Chapter 29: Investment Strategies for Charitable Giving

Capital Raising

Charitable giving is an essential aspect of wealth management and is gaining more significance in the modern world. As a Chartered Wealth Manager (CWM), it is important to understand the various investment strategies for charitable giving to effectively fulfill the philanthropic goals of your clients. One of the most vital components of charitable giving is capital raising, which involves raising funds to donate to charitable organizations or causes. However, capital raising should not be limited to just monetary contributions, but also include other assets such as real estate, securities, and personal property. As a CWM, you have a unique understanding of your client's financial situation and can help them strategize on the most efficient ways to raise capital for charitable purposes. This can involve leveraging tax benefits, such as deductions and exemptions for charitable donations, to minimize the impact on your client's overall financial well-being. You can also assist in creating trust funds or foundations that can help generate a consistent stream of income for charitable giving.

Debt Restructuring

In some cases, individuals or businesses may have a significant amount of debt that can hinder their ability to make substantial charitable contributions. As a CWM, you can provide expertise in debt restructuring to help your clients alleviate their financial burden and make room for charitable giving. This may involve negotiating with creditors to lower interest rates or restructure repayment terms, which can free up funds for charitable contributions. Furthermore, debt restructuring can also involve utilizing assets to settle debts, such as liquidating non-performing assets or refinancing loans. As a CWM, you have the knowledge and skills to analyze your client's portfolio and identify potential assets that can be used to pay off debts and redirect funds towards charitable causes.

Business Expansion

When it comes to charitable giving, business owners have a unique advantage as they can use their business resources to support philanthropic causes. As a CWM, you can assist your business owner clients in strategically expanding their businesses to generate more revenue, which can then be used for charitable giving. This can involve exploring new markets, merging with other companies, or diversifying products and services. Moreover, business expansion can also involve implementing social responsibility initiatives within the company, such as giving a portion of profits to charitable causes or engaging in community service projects. As a CWM, you can guide your clients in developing and executing effective business expansion strategies that align with their philanthropic goals. Charitable giving is not just about donating funds; it's also about making a sustainable impact on society. As a CWM, you have a responsibility to educate your clients on the various investment strategies for charitable giving and how they can make a difference in the world through their wealth. Along with the traditional methods of donating to charities, you can also introduce your clients to impact investing, which involves investing in companies and organizations that have a positive impact on the environment and society. In addition to introducing your clients to impact investing, you can also facilitate networking opportunities for your clients with other like-minded individuals and organizations. This can not only result in increased contributions towards charitable causes but can also foster partnerships and collaborations for more significant impact.

Furthermore, as a CWM, you can also guide your clients in setting up philanthropic events or establishing foundations to promote their charitable goals. In conclusion, as a CWM, you have the privilege of helping your clients make a meaningful impact on society through their wealth. By providing expertise in capital raising, debt restructuring, and business expansion, you can assist your clients in fulfilling their philanthropic goals and leaving a positive legacy. Always remember, charitable giving is not just about the act of giving but also about making a lasting impact on the lives of others.

Chapter 30: Behavioral Strategies for Wealth Management

Managing Emotions

Wealth management is not just about numbers and financial strategies, it also involves managing emotions. As human beings, emotions play a significant role in our decision-making process, including financial decisions. Fear, greed, and overconfidence are some of the common emotions that can have a negative impact on wealth management. The key to successful wealth management is to acknowledge and understand these emotions, and then finding ways to manage them effectively. One of the important emotions to manage is fear. During volatile market conditions, fear can take over and make us act impulsively, leading to negative financial outcomes. The key is to not let fear paralyze you, but instead, take a step back and carefully assess the situation. Seek advice from your trusted financial advisor and focus on the long-term goals of your investment plan. Remember, market fluctuations are a part of the investment journey, and it is important to stay calm and not let emotions take over. On the other hand, greed is an emotion that can cause us to take unnecessary risks in the pursuit of high returns. While it is natural to want to increase our wealth, it is important to have a realistic and rational approach. Be cautious of investment opportunities that promise high returns with low risk. It is always wise to do thorough research and consult with your financial advisor before making any investment decisions.

Behavioral Biases

Behavioral biases are inherent in all of us and can have a significant impact on financial decision-making. These biases can range from confirmation bias, where we seek out information that supports our beliefs, to loss aversion bias, where we feel the pain of losses more than the joy of gains. These biases can cause us to make irrational and impulsive decisions, affecting our wealth management goals. The first step in overcoming behavioral biases is to be aware of them. Recognizing and acknowledging these biases can help us make more rational decisions. Surrounding yourself with a diverse group of individuals with different perspectives can also help challenge your biases and provide a more objective view. Another effective approach in overcoming behavioral biases is to rely on data and analysis rather than emotions. Consult with your financial advisor, who can help you make informed decisions based on factual information and avoid the pitfalls of biased decision-making.

Overcoming Financial Setbacks

Financial setbacks are a part of life, and they can often catch us off guard. These setbacks can be anything from a job loss to a health emergency, sudden market crashes, or unexpected expenses. The key to overcoming these setbacks is to be financially prepared. One of the best ways to prepare for financial setbacks is to have an emergency fund. This fund should ideally cover at least six months of living expenses and should be easily accessible in case of emergencies. It can help you avoid having to sell your investments or taking on debt. It is also important to have a contingency plan in place. Review your investment portfolio with your financial advisor and discuss potential scenarios where you may need to make adjustments. This can help you make more informed decisions in times of uncertainty. Moreover, having a strong long-term investment plan in place can help mitigate the impact of financial setbacks and keep you on track towards your wealth management goals. In conclusion, managing emotions, overcoming behavioral biases, and being prepared for financial setbacks are key behavioral strategies for successful wealth management. Being aware of our emotions and biases, seeking professional guidance, and having contingency plans in place can help us make better financial decisions and achieve our financial goals. Remember to stay calm, stay focused, and have faith in your long-term investment plan.

Chapter 31: Strategic Exit Planning for Investors

Rebalancing Strategies

As a Chartered Wealth Manager, it is your responsibility to constantly monitor and rebalance your clients' investment portfolios. This process involves selling assets that have exceeded their target allocation and purchasing assets that have fallen below their target allocation. The goal of rebalancing is to maintain the intended risk level of the portfolio and prevent it from becoming too heavily skewed towards one asset class. One common rebalancing strategy is calendar-based, where portfolios are rebalanced every six months or every year. However, there are other rebalancing strategies that can be more effective, such as threshold-based or opportunistic rebalancing. Threshold-based rebalancing involves setting a predetermined threshold for each asset class, and when it deviates from its target allocation by a certain percentage, it triggers a rebalancing. Opportunistic rebalancing, on the other hand, takes advantage of market movements to buy or sell assets, rather than following a predefined schedule.

Performance Evaluation

Evaluating the performance of an investment portfolio is crucial for a CWM. It not only helps to track the progress towards financial goals, but it also enables you to determine the effectiveness of the investment strategy and make adjustments if necessary. When evaluating performance, it is essential to consider the time horizon, risk appetite, and goals of the client. Short-term fluctuations in the market can often lead to misleading performance metrics, so it is important to focus on longer-term results. Additionally, benchmarking can be a useful tool in performance evaluation. This involves comparing the portfolio's return to a relevant market index to determine if the investment strategy is outperforming or underperforming.

Benchmarking

Benchmarking is a method of comparing the performance of an investment portfolio to a specific market index or a blend of indexes that reflect the overall market. This allows you to determine if the portfolio is achieving the desired return and risk level based on the market conditions. While benchmarking is a useful tool, it is crucial to choose an appropriate benchmark that aligns with the client's investment objectives and risk tolerance. For example, if the client has a conservative risk tolerance, comparing their portfolio to a benchmark that is heavily weighted towards equity investments may not be an accurate representation of performance. In addition to using traditional benchmarks, there are also alternative benchmarks that can be used, such as peer group comparisons or absolute return targets. Peer group comparisons involve comparing the portfolio to other similar investment portfolios to determine if it is performing in line with its peers. Absolute return targets, on the other hand, involve setting a specific return goal for the portfolio and evaluating its performance based on that target.

Unconventional Strategies

While traditional rebalancing, performance evaluation, and benchmarking strategies are effective, it is crucial for a CWM to think outside the box and explore unconventional strategies as well. This includes considering unconventional assets, such as commodities or real estate, as part of the investment portfolio. Alternative investments can provide diversification and potentially higher returns, but they also come with their own risks, so thorough research and understanding are essential before incorporating them into a portfolio. Another unconventional strategy is taking a tactical approach to investing. This means having a flexible investment strategy that can adjust to current market conditions. This approach involves proactively managing market volatility and taking advantage of opportunities as they arise. It requires a deep understanding of the market and the ability to make quick and informed decisions.

The Role of a CWM

As a Chartered Wealth Manager, it is crucial to constantly stay updated on market trends, new investment strategies, and regulatory changes to provide the best possible services to your clients. It is also essential to think creatively and explore unconventional strategies that can potentially enhance portfolio performance and mitigate risk. Strategic exit planning is a crucial aspect of wealth management that is often overlooked. It involves having a plan in place for when to exit certain investments and how to do so in a manner that aligns with the client's financial goals. As a CWM, it is your responsibility to guide your clients through this process and ensure that their investments are aligned with their personal and financial objectives. From rebalancing strategies to performance evaluation and benchmarking, the role of a CWM in wealth management is multifaceted and requires a sophisticated, artistic, cheerful, and cultured approach. By implementing unconventional strategies and constantly adjusting to market conditions, a CWM can help their clients achieve their financial goals and build long-term wealth.

Chapter 32: Evaluating Investment Performance

Risk-adjusted Return

When evaluating investment performance, it is important to look not only at the returns but also at the level of risk associated with those returns. This is where risk-adjusted return comes into play. Risk-adjusted return is a measure of how much return an investment generates for each unit of risk taken. In other words, it takes into account the level of risk involved in obtaining a return. Investors often make the mistake of solely focusing on the returns, but this can be misleading as higher returns do not always mean a better investment. It's important to consider the level of risk involved to get a more accurate understanding of the investment's performance.

Alpha and Beta

When evaluating investment performance, it is also important to understand the concepts of alpha and beta. These two terms are often used in relation to the Capital Asset Pricing Model (CAPM) and are measures of an investment's risk-adjusted return. Alpha is a measure of an investment's return that is above or below the market return. . A positive alpha indicates that the investment has outperformed the market, while a negative alpha means it has underperformed. This can help investors identify whether a particular investment is doing well due to its own merits or if it is just benefiting from a bullish market. On the other hand, beta measures an investment's volatility in relation to the market. A beta of 1 indicates that the investment moves in line with the market, while a beta of less than 1 means that it is less volatile than the market. A beta of more than 1 indicates that the investment is more volatile than the market. Understanding the beta of an investment can help investors determine its level of risk and how it may perform in different market conditions.

Sharpe Ratio

The Sharpe ratio is another tool used in evaluating investment performance. It was developed by Nobel Prize-winning economist William F. Sharpe and measures an investment's excess return per unit of risk. In simple terms, it tells us how much return an investment generates for each unit of risk taken. A higher Sharpe ratio indicates a better risk-adjusted return. It is calculated by taking the investment's return and subtracting the risk-free rate (such as a government bond rate) and dividing it by the investment's standard deviation (a measure of volatility). This can help investors compare investments with different levels of risk and determine their performance relative to the level of risk taken.

Uncommon Considerations

When evaluating investment performance, it's important to consider both mathematical measures and qualitative factors. While numbers can tell us a lot, they do not always paint the full picture. For example, a stock with a high beta may appear to be riskier, but it could actually be a strong performer due to its unique business model or industry. Additionally, it's important to consider an investment's performance over a longer time horizon rather than just short-term results. A higher return over a short period may be due to luck or a temporary market trend, but a consistent track record of outperforming the market is a better indicator of a strong investment. Cultural and political factors can also play a role in the performance of investments, especially in international markets. Understanding these factors and how they may impact an investment can provide valuable insight when evaluating performance.

Artistic Analysis

Investment performance evaluation is often seen as a purely analytical and mathematical process, but it can also be likened to a form of art. Just as artists use various techniques to create a masterpiece, investors also use different tools and methods to evaluate performance and make informed decisions. Similar to how an artist may experiment with different colors and mediums, investors must also be open to using different measures and considering various factors in their evaluation process. This allows for a more well-rounded and accurate analysis of an investment's performance.

Cheerful Conclusion

Evaluating investment performance is a crucial part of the wealth management process, and understanding concepts like risk-adjusted return, alpha and beta, and the Sharpe ratio can greatly enhance one's ability to make informed investment decisions. But it's important to remember not to rely solely on numbers and to consider qualitative factors and a longer-term perspective. As we've discovered, evaluating performance can be both an analytical and artistic process that requires an open mind and a willingness to think outside the box. By incorporating all of these elements, we can truly make informed and prosperous investments.

Chapter 33: Strategic Exit Planning for Investors

Exit Strategies

When it comes to investing, most people focus on the exciting process of buying and managing their investments. However, it is equally important to have a well-thought-out exit strategy. Exiting an investment can be just as important as entering one, if not more so. As a Chartered Wealth Manager (CWM), it is your responsibility to guide your clients through the process of developing a strategic exit plan. There are many potential exit strategies available to investors and each one should be carefully considered depending on the specific investment and the goals of the investor. Common exit strategies include selling to another investor, going public on the stock market, and liquidation. However, there are also more creative and uncommon options that may be more suitable for certain situations. One uncommon exit strategy is the management buyout (MBO). This involves the current management team purchasing the business from the owners. This can be a viable option for smaller businesses in which the management team has played a key role in the success of the company. This also allows the current owners to exit the business without having to look for an outside buyer. Another uncommon option is an employee stock ownership plan (ESOP). This involves creating a trust that will own shares of the company on behalf of the employees. This option can be beneficial for both the owners and the employees, as it allows the employees to have a stake in the company and the owners to gradually transfer control while still receiving financial benefits.

Selling a Business

For many entrepreneurs and business owners, their business is not just a source of income but is also a major part of their identity. As such, selling a business can be a difficult decision and process. As a CWM, you must guide your clients through the emotional and financial aspects of selling a business. One important aspect of selling a business is finding the right buyer. This not only means finding someone who is willing to pay a fair price, but also someone who will maintain the values and vision of the business. It is important for the current owners to carefully consider their options and not rush into a sale simply for the sake of making a quick exit. Valuing a business can also be a complex process. It is crucial to have a clear understanding of the financials and potential growth of the business in order to determine a fair price. This is where a

CWM can provide valuable insight and support in the decision-making process.

Planning for Change in Personal Circumstances

Life is unpredictable and circumstances can change at any moment. As a CWM, part of your role is to help your clients plan for potential changes in their personal circumstances that may affect their investments. One important consideration is the issue of succession planning. This involves planning for the transfer of wealth, assets and responsibilities to the next generation. This can be a complex process, especially for high net worth individuals with complex assets and family dynamics. By helping your clients navigate this process, you can ensure that their legacy and wealth is preserved for future generations. Another aspect to consider is the impact of major life events, such as marriage, divorce, or the birth of children, on investments. It is important for investors to update their financial plans and make necessary adjustments as their personal circumstances change. As a CWM, you can assist your clients in adapting their investments to align with their new goals and priorities. In addition to these considerations, it is also important to plan for unexpected events, such as illness or disability. This involves having appropriate insurance coverage and creating contingency plans to mitigate potential financial impacts.

Conclusion

As a Chartered Wealth Manager, it is your responsibility to guide your clients through the process of developing an exit plan that aligns with their individual goals and circumstances. This involves evaluating all available exit strategies and considering uncommon options that may be more suitable for certain situations. You must also provide support and guidance during the emotional process of selling a business and help your clients plan for potential changes in their personal circumstances. By doing so, you can ensure that your clients have a well-thought-out exit plan in place to protect their investments and achieve their long-term financial goals.

Chapter 34: International Wealth Management

Tax Implications

When it comes to international wealth management, one of the key considerations for investors is to understand the tax implications of their investments. While it may be tempting to simply focus on the potential returns, it is important to also consider the tax laws and regulations of different countries. For individuals with significant wealth, tax planning can play a crucial role in maintaining and growing their assets. This is especially true when investing internationally, as different countries have varying tax laws and reporting requirements. Without proper consideration, investors may find themselves facing unexpected tax liabilities. One strategy for managing taxes in international investments is to consider jurisdictions with favorable tax laws. These can include countries with lower tax rates, tax treaties that offer favorable terms, or tax-free investment options. Another consideration is to structure investments in a way that minimizes tax liabilities. For example, using tax-advantaged accounts or investing through a trust can help reduce taxes on investment returns. It is important for investors to work closely with a qualified tax professional to ensure that their international investments are compliant with tax laws and to minimize potential tax liabilities.

Diversification Strategies

Diversification is a fundamental principle of successful wealth management, and this is especially true when investing internationally. By diversifying across different countries and regions, investors can reduce their exposure to any one country or market and potentially increase overall returns. One strategy for international diversification is through index funds or exchange-traded funds (ETFs), which provide exposure to multiple countries and markets in a single investment. This can be an efficient and cost-effective way to achieve diversification in an international portfolio. Another strategy is to invest in specific industries or sectors in different countries, rather than just broad market indexes. This can provide exposure to specific areas experiencing growth or opportunity, and potentially enhance overall returns. It is important for investors to carefully consider their risk tolerance and investment goals when developing a diversification strategy for their international investments. A balanced and diversified portfolio can help mitigate risk and optimize returns over the long term.

Regulatory Considerations

International investing also comes with regulatory considerations that investors need to be aware of. Each country has its own set of laws and regulations governing investments, and these can vary significantly. Before investing internationally, investors should research the regulatory environment of the country they are considering. This can include everything from the process for acquiring assets, to reporting and compliance requirements, to potential restrictions on foreign investments. Additionally, it is important to understand the stability and overall economic health of a country before investing. Political turmoil, economic instability, or trade disputes can all have a significant impact on investments. Investors should also be aware of any potential currency risks when investing internationally. Fluctuations in exchange rates can have a significant impact on investment returns, so it is important to carefully consider this when choosing countries and currencies for investments. In conclusion, international wealth management offers a myriad of opportunities for investors.

However, it also comes with unique challenges and considerations that must be carefully navigated. By understanding tax implications, implementing diversification strategies, and considering regulatory factors, investors can make informed and strategic decisions to help grow and protect their wealth on a global scale. Working with a qualified wealth manager who has experience in international investments can help ensure that investors are well-informed and well-positioned to achieve their financial goals.

Chapter 35: International Wealth Management – Ensuring Security in a Digital World

In today's world, where everything is just a click away, wealth management is no exception. With the rise of online advisory services, mobile banking, and the increasing importance of cybersecurity, international wealth management has undergone a significant transformation. As a CWM, it is essential to understand and navigate these digital advancements to ensure the security and success of your clients' wealth management strategies. Let's dive deeper into these areas and uncover some uncommon facts about them.

Online Advisory – The Future of Wealth Management

Online advisory services use digital platforms and tools to assist clients with their investment decisions, financial planning, and portfolio management. This approach has gained immense popularity among clients due to its convenience, cost-effectiveness, and accessibility. As a CWM, it is crucial to understand the power of these online tools and how to leverage them to provide efficient services to your clients. However, here's an unusual fact – while online advisory services are increasingly popular among younger generations, affluent individuals are still more likely to seek traditional face-to-face services. This highlights the importance of maintaining a balance between traditional and digital methods in international wealth management.

Mobile Banking – Convenience at Your Fingertips

Mobile banking has revolutionized the financial industry, including wealth management. With just a few taps on their smartphones, clients can now access their accounts, track investments, and even make transactions, all in real-time. The convenience and speed of mobile banking have made it an integral part of modern wealth management strategies. But here's an artistic twist – while mobile banking offers significant advantages, it also comes with its cybersecurity risks. As a CWM, it is essential to educate your clients on the importance of securing their devices and keeping their financial information safe. This can be achieved through strong passwords, regularly updating software, and avoiding public Wi-Fi networks while handling financial matters.

Cybersecurity – Protecting Your Clients' Wealth

With the increasing use of technology in wealth management, cybersecurity has become a top priority. Clients entrust their most valuable asset, their wealth, to their CWM, making it crucial to safeguard it from cyber threats. To maintain this trust, CWMs must stay updated on the ever-evolving cybersecurity landscape and take preventative measures to protect their clients' wealth. Here's an uncommon fact – cybercriminals are no longer just targeting large corporations and financial institutions. Wealthy individuals are also at risk of cyber attacks, making it essential for CWMs to implement robust cybersecurity protocols. These may include secure online platforms, encrypted communication channels, and regular security audits. By taking these steps, CWMs can ensure the continued safety and success of their clients' wealth management strategies.

Maintaining a Balance – Tradition, and Innovation

In the rapidly evolving world of international wealth management, it is crucial to maintain a balance between traditional and modern approaches. While digital advancements offer convenience and efficiency, the personal touch and expertise of a CWM are irreplaceable. By embracing both traditional and digital methods, CWMs can provide a comprehensive and tailored approach to wealth management that suits their clients' needs. But here's a cheerful fact – with the rise of technology and online tools, CWMs can now better serve a larger pool of clients, regardless of their location. This has opened up new opportunities for international wealth management, making it possible to provide top-notch services to individuals worldwide.

Conclusion

As we've seen, the digital landscape has significantly impacted the field of international wealth management. Online advisory services, mobile banking, and cybersecurity are just some of the areas that have undergone a significant transformation. As a CWM, it is vital to stay updated and adapt to these changes to provide the best services possible to your clients. By finding a balance between tradition and innovation, CWMs can ensure the security and success of their clients' wealth management strategies in this digital world.

Chapter 36: International Wealth Management

International wealth management is a constantly evolving field, as wealth managers are continually faced with new global events, trade wars, and political instability that can greatly impact their clients' investments. As a Chartered Wealth Manager (CWM), it is important to stay informed and adapt to these changes in order to effectively manage your clients' wealth.

Global Events

One of the key aspects of international wealth management is monitoring and assessing global events that can affect the financial markets. These events can range from natural disasters and political crises to economic downturns and pandemics. As a CWM, it is essential to stay up-to-date with current events and understand how they can impact your clients' investments. For instance, the recent COVID-19 pandemic has caused unprecedented disruption in the global economy and financial markets. Many businesses have suffered, leading to a decline in stock prices and an increase in volatility. As a wealth manager, it is crucial to reassess your clients' investment portfolios and make necessary adjustments to mitigate the risks associated with these events.

Trade Wars

Trade wars can have a significant impact on investment strategies, as they often result in tariffs and other trade barriers being imposed on goods and services between countries. This can lead to changes in currency values and adjustments in trade agreements, which can directly affect various industries and companies. As a CWM, it is crucial to understand the potential effects of trade wars on your clients' investments. This includes staying informed about current trade negotiations and their potential outcomes. By monitoring these events closely, you can make informed decisions about your clients' investment portfolios to mitigate any potential risks.

Political Instability

Political instability is another factor that can greatly impact the global economy and financial markets. Changes in government policies, elections, and shifts in power can cause uncertainty and volatility in the markets. It is essential for wealth managers to understand the potential effects of political instability on their clients' investments. For example, Brexit has been a significant source of political instability in recent years, with the UK's decision to leave the European Union causing uncertainty in global markets. As a CWM, it is crucial to monitor political events and attitudes towards economic policies in order to make well-informed investment decisions for your clients. Uncommon Gems Managing international wealth also means understanding the cultural and social aspects of your clients' investments. The preferences and values of individuals in different countries may greatly impact their investment decisions. As a CWM, it is important to consider these factors when creating investment strategies for your clients. Additionally, language barriers and varying tax regulations in different countries can also present challenges for managing international wealth. A CWM must be adaptable and resourceful in navigating these uncommon obstacles.

The Role of Technology

Technology has greatly impacted the field of wealth management, making it easier to manage and monitor international investments. With advancements in digital platforms and tools, CWMs can now effectively diversify and manage their clients' portfolios across different countries and regions. Technology has also made it easier to access and analyze data, allowing wealth managers to make data-driven decisions for their clients' investments. However, with the rise of financial technology (FinTech), it is crucial for CWMs to stay informed and utilize these tools effectively in order to remain competitive in the global marketplace.

Staying Culturally Sensitive

With international wealth management, it is important to be culturally sensitive and aware of social customs and practices in different countries. CWMs must understand the cultural nuances and norms of the markets they are operating in, as well as the preferences and values of their clients. For instance, investing in certain industries or companies may be frowned upon in some cultures, and it is important for wealth managers to consider these factors when creating investment strategies for their clients. A culturally sensitive approach can help build stronger client relationships and improve client satisfaction.

Conclusion

International wealth management is a complex and dynamic field that requires constant adaptation and understanding of global events, trade wars, and political instability, as well as cultural sensitivity and the role of technology. As a CWM, staying informed and adaptable is essential in effectively managing your clients' investments and ensuring their long-term financial success. By staying ahead of these uncommon factors, wealth managers can continue to provide valuable guidance and expertise to their clients' international wealth portfolios.

Chapter 37: Managing Unexpected Wealth

Inheritance

Managing unexpected wealth from an inheritance can be a complex and emotional experience. While it may bring a sense of financial security, it can also come with its own set of challenges. One of the biggest challenges is managing the emotional attachment to the inherited assets. These assets may hold sentimental value, making it difficult to make sound financial decisions. It is important to work closely with a financial advisor to develop a plan for the inherited assets that aligns with your financial goals.

Windfall

A windfall is any unexpected, large sum of money that comes into your possession. This could include lottery winnings, legal settlements, or unexpected bonuses. While a windfall may seem like a dream come true, it is important to resist the urge to spend it all at once. It is wise to take the time to carefully plan how to use the windfall to secure your financial future. This could include paying off debts, investing in retirement accounts, or setting up an emergency fund.

Sale of a Business

Selling a business can bring in a significant amount of unexpected wealth. However, this can also come with a great deal of stress and uncertainty. It is important to carefully plan and consider all potential outcomes before making any decisions. Seeking the guidance of a financial advisor can help you navigate through this process and make informed decisions regarding how to manage the wealth from the sale of your business.

Uncommon Considerations

While managing unexpected wealth, it is important to consider the impact it may have on your taxes. Depending on how the wealth is received, it may be subject to income tax or capital gains tax. It is crucial to work with a tax professional to understand the tax implications and make strategic decisions to minimize the impact on your wealth. Another key consideration is the impact of this sudden wealth on your lifestyle. It is tempting to immediately upgrade your living standards, but it is important to think long-term and avoid making impulsive decisions. Setting a budget and financial plan with the help of a financial advisor can ensure the wealth is used wisely and supports your financial goals.

The Role of a CWM

Thoroughly managing unexpected wealth requires a professional and strategic approach, which is where a Chartered Wealth Manager (CWM) can play a crucial role. A CWM is trained in creating and implementing comprehensive wealth management strategies that align with your unique financial goals and circumstances. They can offer valuable guidance and advice to help navigate through the challenges of managing unexpected wealth. They can also assist in developing a plan to preserve and grow the wealth for future generations. In conclusion, managing unexpected wealth can be a daunting task, but with the right support and guidance, it can pave the way for a more secure financial future. Seeking the advice of a CWM can help ensure that the wealth is managed strategically and aligns with your long-term financial goals. By carefully planning and making informed decisions, you can make the most of these unexpected sources of wealth and secure a brighter financial future.

Chapter 38: Managing Financial Crises

Financial crises are a part of the economic cycle that cannot be avoided. They come in different forms and can have a significant impact on individuals, businesses, and even the global economy. It is a time of uncertainty, panic, and fear as people struggle to safeguard their wealth and assets. In this chapter, we will explore the different types of financial crises and how a CWM can help individuals and businesses manage their wealth in such difficult times.

Recession

A recession is a period of general economic decline, typically defined as a decline in GDP for two consecutive quarters. It is a significant part of the economic cycle and can have far-reaching consequences. During a recession, consumer spending decreases, businesses may lay off employees, and stock markets tumble. It is a time of uncertainty, and people tend to become more cautious with their spending and investment decisions. As a CWM, it is essential to understand how a recession can affect your clients' wealth. It is a time when people may need to make significant adjustments to their financial plan to weather the storm. This can include reevaluating their investments, looking for safe-haven assets, and reassessing their risk tolerance. It is also crucial for a CWM to provide emotional support and guidance to their clients during this challenging time.

Market Downturn

A market downturn refers to a sharp decline in the value of securities in a particular market or asset class. While recessions can trigger market downturns, they can also occur without a significant economic decline. Market downturns can be caused by a variety of factors, such as political turmoil, natural disasters, or unexpected events like a pandemic. For individuals, market downturns can be a time of high anxiety, especially for those who have a significant portion of their wealth invested in the stock market. As a CWM, it is crucial to have a diversified investment strategy in place to help minimize the impact of market downturns. This can include investing in different asset classes, such as fixed-income securities, commodities, or real estate. Diversification can help reduce volatility and protect wealth during market downturns.

Moreover, it is essential to have a long-term investment perspective during market downturns. It is natural for investors to panic and want to sell their investments when the market is in a freefall. However, as a CWM, it is your responsibility to remind clients that market downturns are temporary, and history has shown that markets tend to recover. Selling investments during a market downturn can result in locking in losses and missing out on future growth opportunities.

Bankruptcy

Bankruptcy refers to a legal process of financial insolvency, where a person or business is unable to repay their debts. It is often a last resort for individuals or businesses who are struggling with their finances. Bankruptcy can be caused by many factors, such as a sudden job loss, high medical bills, or poor financial management.

When a client is facing bankruptcy, they may feel like they have lost all control over their finances. As a CWM, it is important to offer support and guidance to help your client navigate this difficult situation. This can include helping them create a budget to manage their expenses, exploring debt consolidation options, and providing financial education to help them make better financial decisions in the future.

Moreover, a CWM can also play a crucial role in helping clients rebuild their wealth after bankruptcy. This can include creating a new financial plan that takes into account their current situation and future goals. It may also involve helping them invest wisely to rebuild their savings and investing reserves for emergency situations.

Unconventional Strategies for Managing Financial Crises

While the traditional strategies of diversification and long-term investing are essential during a financial crisis, there are also some unconventional strategies that a CWM can explore to help manage their clients' wealth. These strategies may not be suitable for every client, but they can offer unique solutions in specific situations.
One unconventional strategy is to invest in distressed assets. These are assets that have significantly declined in value but have the potential for a turnaround. Distressed

assets can include distressed real estate, stocks of struggling companies, and even art collections. While this strategy comes with a higher level of risk, it can also offer significant growth potential if the assets bounce back.

Another unconventional strategy is to create a cash reserve fund for emergency situations. This fund can be in the form of low-risk investments, such as high-yield savings accounts, money market funds, or short-term government bonds. This fund can provide a cushion for clients during a financial crisis, allowing them to manage their expenses without liquidating their long-term investments.

Lastly, investing in alternative assets, such as private equity, hedge funds, and venture capital can also provide diversification and potentially higher returns during a financial crisis. However, these investments are typically only available to accredited investors and come with a higher level of risk.

In Conclusion

Managing financial crises is an integral part of a CWM's role. It requires not only a deep understanding of the markets and economic trends but also the ability to provide emotional support and guidance to clients during times of uncertainty. By being proactive, having a diverse investment strategy, and exploring unconventional strategies, a CWM can help their clients weather the storm and come out stronger in the end. Remember, the key to managing financial crises is preparation, communication, and trust between a CWM and their clients. By working together, clients can feel secure in the knowledge that their wealth is in good hands, no matter what challenges may come their way.

.

Chapter 39: The Future of Wealth Management

As we look towards the future of wealth management, we can see that the industry is constantly evolving and adapting to changing times. In this chapter, we will explore some of the trends, innovations, and challenges that are shaping the future of wealth management.

Trends

One of the major trends in wealth management is the increasing use of technology. With the rise of robo-advisors and online wealth management platforms, investors now have more options than ever before. These technological advancements have made it easier and more accessible for individuals to manage their wealth, and have also allowed for more personalized and efficient investment strategies.

Another trend in wealth management is the focus on environmentally and socially responsible investing. As the global awareness of climate change and social issues grows, investors are becoming more conscious of where their money is being invested. This trend has led to the rise of green and ethical investment options, providing investors with the opportunity to make a positive impact while still achieving their financial goals.

Lastly, we are seeing an increasing trend of international wealth management. With the ease of global communication and trading, investors are looking beyond their local markets and diversifying their portfolios internationally. This presents unique challenges and opportunities for wealth managers, as they navigate different regulations, cultural differences, and economic landscapes.

Innovations

Technology is once again at the forefront of innovations in wealth management. Artificial intelligence, machine learning, and big data are being utilized to analyze market trends and make more informed investment decisions. This allows wealth managers to stay ahead of the curve and provide their clients with more value-added services.

Another exciting innovation in wealth management is the use of blockchain technology. This decentralized digital ledger system has the potential to revolutionize the way assets are managed and traded, making it more efficient, secure, and transparent. As this technology continues to develop, we can expect to see more applications in the wealth management industry. Virtual wealth management is also gaining popularity, especially in light of the global pandemic. With the ability to conduct meetings, consultations, and transactions online, investors no longer have to be limited by location. This not only brings convenience but also provides access to a wider range of investment opportunities and expertise.

Challenges

While the future of wealth management is bright, there are also challenges that need to be addressed. Cybersecurity is a major concern, as technology becomes more integral to the wealth management process. Wealth management firms need to invest in robust security measures to protect sensitive data and ensure the trust of their clients. Another challenge is the increasing complexity of regulations. As the financial industry becomes more globalized, there are multiple layers of regulations to navigate, which can be time-consuming and costly. Wealth managers need to stay on top of these regulations to ensure compliance and avoid any legal repercussions.

Lastly, the rise of self-directed investing has created competition for traditional wealth management firms. With the abundance of information and resources available online, investors are more empowered to manage their own investments. Wealth managers must find ways to differentiate and add value to their services to remain relevant in this changing landscape.

In conclusion, the future of wealth management is marked by technological advancements, socially and environmentally responsible investing, and global expansion. While there are challenges to overcome, the industry is constantly evolving and adapting to provide the best services for clients. The role of a CWM will continue to be crucial in navigating this complex and ever-changing landscape, providing expertise, guidance, and personalized solutions for their clients' wealth management needs.

Practice Exam Questions

Book 1 - Wealth Management Strategies

Practice Question Set 1

1. What are the benefits of pursuing a Chartered Wealth Manager (CWM) designation?

2. What is estate planning?

3. What is the role of a CWM in wealth management?

4. What is the importance of estate planning?

5. Name three types of clients for wealth management.

6. What is the Code of Conduct for CWMs?

7. What is asset allocation?

8. What is risk management in portfolio management?

9. What are the steps of the estate planning process?

10. Name three types of taxes that may impact an individual's wealth.

11. How can tax efficient investing help minimize tax liability?

12. What is the role of client relationship management in wealth management?

13. Name five common investment vehicles.

14. What is the difference between a trust and a will?

15. What is the legal framework for estate and trust law?

16. What is the role of a CWM in tax planning?

17. How can a CWM build trust with their clients?

18. What are three types of alternative investments?

19. What is the fiduciary duty of a CWM?

20. What is the difference between risk tolerance and risk capacity?

21. What is the purpose of diversification in portfolio management?

22. What are the goals of estate planning?

23. How can wealth management strategies differ for high net worth individuals compared to other clients?

24. What is an uncommon approach to asset allocation?

25. What is the purpose of tax planning in wealth management?

26. How does estate planning address potential legal complications?

27. Name three types of risk that investors should consider in portfolio management.

28. What is the role of professionalism in the Code of Conduct for CWMs?

29. How can clients benefit from a CWM's knowledge of alternative investments?

30. What is a common tax strategy for minimizing estate taxes?

31. What are some common ways that individuals can minimize tax liabilities?

32. What is a potential risk of investing in alternative investments?

33. What is the purpose of the estate planning process?

34. Name two benefits of estate planning.

35. How can a CWM effectively communicate with clients?

36. What is the role of insurance in wealth management?

37. How does tax planning differ from tax preparation?

38. How can a CWM help clients with business succession planning?

39. Name two strategies for minimizing risk in portfolio management.

40. What is the importance of staying up-to-date on tax laws and regulations?

41. What is a potential benefit of investing in real estate?

42. What is a potential drawback of investing in private equity?

43. What is a potential challenge of estate planning for blended families?

44. How can estate planning help avoid potential family conflicts?

45. How can a CWM assist clients in diversifying their portfolio?

46. What are the potential benefits of investing in alternative investments?

47. What is a common concern for high net worth individuals when it comes to estate planning?

48. How can a CWM address potential conflicts of interest?

49. What is a potential benefit of investing in hedge funds?

50. How can CWMs help clients plan for unexpected events, such as disability or long-term care needs?

Practice Question Set 2

1. What is the primary purpose of a financial plan?

2. What are the key components of a financial plan?

3. What is the role of asset allocation in a financial plan?

4. How can risk be managed in a financial plan?

5. What are the three types of risk?

6. Why is tax planning an important aspect of a financial plan?

7. What is the purpose of retirement planning?

8. What is the primary source of retirement income for most Americans?

9. What is an annuity and how does it work?

10. What is long-term care insurance and why is it important in retirement planning?

11. How can tax planning be integrated into retirement planning?

12. What is the goal of estate planning?

13. What is an index fund and how does it work?

14. What are the advantages of passive investing?

15. What is fundamental analysis and how is it used in investment analysis?

16. How does technical analysis differ from fundamental analysis?

17. What is a derivative and how is it used in portfolio management?

18. What are some strategies for valuing investments?

19. What is succession planning and why is it important in estate planning for business owners?

20. What is the purpose of a buy-sell agreement?

21. What are the types of insurance that can help manage risks for corporate and executive compensation?

22. What are some alternative investments that can potentially provide higher returns but also have higher risks?

23. How can currency risk be managed in global investing?

24. What are structured notes and how do they work?

25. What are the benefits of using structured notes in a portfolio?

26. What are certificates of deposit and how do they work?

27. What is market risk and how can it be managed?

28. What is liquidity risk and how can it be managed?

29. What is credit risk and how can it be managed?

30. What is family governance and why is it important in estate planning?

31. How can behavioral biases impact decision-making in investing?

32. What are common biases that investors should be aware of?

33. What are some uncommon approaches to advanced retirement strategies?

34. How can derivatives be used to manage risks in a portfolio?

35. What is the difference between single-stock futures and stock options?

36. Why is it important to consider the tax implications when choosing investments?

37. What is a convertible bond and how is it different from a regular bond?

38. How can technical analysis be used to identify potential trading opportunities?

39. How can family businesses use succession planning to ensure their continued success?

40. What are some common strategies for valuing a business?

41. How can diversity and inclusion help manage risks in corporate leadership?

Practice Question Set 3

1. What are the key components of a typical financial plan?

2. What are some common indicators used in portfolio performance measurement?

3. How can a wealth manager help clients with tax planning?

4. What is the purpose of diversification in investment planning?

5. What are the potential benefits and risks of real estate investments?

6. What is the importance of setting goals in financial planning?

7. How can alternative investments, such as private equity, add value to a portfolio?

8. What factors should be considered when creating a legacy plan?

9. How can hedging be used as a tax planning strategy?

10. What are the potential risks associated with volatile assets, such as cryptocurrencies?

11. How can a private foundation be used as a charitable giving strategy?

12. What are some potential benefits of using technology in performance measurement?

13. What is the purpose of disaster planning in wealth management?

14. How can understanding investor psychology benefit wealth management practices?

15. How can an investor maximize their business value?

16. What is the role of asset allocation in retirement investment planning?

17. How can a wealth manager help clients generate income in retirement?

18. What are some potential benefits of using mission statements in wealth management?

19. How can a donor-advised fund be used for charitable giving?

20. What are some potential cybersecurity risks for wealth managers?

21. How can a wealth manager help clients build wealth outside of their business?

22. How can decision-making be influenced by emotions and biases?

23. What are some benefits of using goal setting in financial planning?

24. How can tracking error measure the performance of a portfolio?

25. What is the impact of inflation on long-term financial planning?

26. How does estate planning help protect an individual's assets?

27. What are the potential advantages of investing in commodities?

28. How can rebalancing be used to manage risk in a portfolio?

29. What factors should be considered when selecting a portfolio benchmark?

30. What is the role of risk management in a financial plan?

31. How can a wealth manager help clients diversify their investments?

32. What is the role of legacy planning in wealth management?

33. How can the owner of a privately-held business maximize their wealth?

34. What are some potential risks of investing in hedge funds?

35. How can legacy planning benefit from the involvement of the next generation?

36. What are some potential benefits of using mission statements in wealth management?

37. How can a wealth manager help clients manage long-term care considerations?

38. What is the advantage of using a benchmark to measure portfolio performance?

39. How can advanced tax planning techniques, such as charitable trusts, benefit wealth management?

40. How can a wealth manager help clients rebalance their portfolio?

41. What are the benefits of using risk-adjusted returns in performance measurement?

42. What is the role of diversification in managing risk in a portfolio?

43. How can a wealth manager help clients with hedging strategies?

44. What are the potential benefits and risks of investing in art?

45. How can disaster planning help protect a client's wealth?

46. What are some common investment strategies used in retirement planning?

47. How can advanced portfolio performance measurement benefit from technology?

48. What are some risks associated with investing in private equity?

49. How can goal setting benefit financial planning?

50. What is the potential impact of investment decisions on taxes in wealth management?

Book 2 - Ethical and Regulatory Framework

Practice Question Set 1

1. What is the role of a CWM in the finance industry?

2. What are some job opportunities available for a CWM?

3. What is the importance of a CWM in the finance industry?

4. How have the landscape and trends in wealth management changed over time?

5. What is the history of the Chartered Wealth Manager designation?

6. How has the CWM designation grown over the years?

7. What are some current trends in wealth management?

8. What are the three key areas of focus in wealth management?

9. What is the difference between traditional and alternative investments?

10. What is the difference between active and passive investment strategies?

11. What are the two main objectives of investing?

12. What is risk tolerance in wealth management?

13. How does diversification help in managing risk?

14. What are the three main asset classes in portfolio construction?

15. What is an uncommon factor in portfolio construction?

16. What is company analysis in investment strategies?

17. What is industry analysis in investment strategies?

18. What is macroeconomic analysis in investment strategies?

19. How do these three types of analysis help in uncovering uncommon investment opportunities?

20. What are the three stages of fundamental analysis?

21. What is charting in fundamental analysis?

22. Name one technical indicator used in fundamental analysis.

23. What are patterns in fundamental analysis?

24. How does behavioral finance explain the impact of psychological biases on wealth management?

25. What is decision making in behavioral finance?

26. How can understanding market sentiments help in wealth management?

27. What is an uncommon knowledge in behavioral finance?

28. Why is goal setting important in wealth management?

29. What is budgeting in the context of wealth management?

30. What is the importance of retirement planning in wealth management?

31. What is the Chartered Wealth Manager (CWM) certification?

32. Where can a CWM work?

33. How does the CWM designation benefit professionals in the finance industry?

34. What is the historical significance of the CWM designation?

35. How has the popularity of the CWM designation changed over the years?

36. What is a current trend in wealth management?

37. What are the three main areas of focus in wealth management?

38. What is the difference between traditional and alternative investments?

39. What is the difference between active and passive investment strategies?

40. What are the two main objectives of investing?

41. What is risk tolerance in wealth management?

42. How does diversification help in managing risk?

43. What are the three main asset classes in portfolio construction?

44. What is an uncommon factor in portfolio construction?

45. What is company analysis in investment strategies?

46. What is industry analysis in investment strategies?

47. What is macroeconomic analysis in investment strategies?

48. How do these three types of analysis help in uncovering uncommon investment opportunities?

49. What are the three stages of fundamental analysis?

50. What is charting in fundamental analysis?

Practice Question Set 2

1. What is the main objective of wealth management?

2. What is the role of a Certified Wealth Manager (CWM) in the field of wealth management?

3. What are the three pillars of wealth management?

4. What are some factors that influence a client's risk tolerance?

5. How can a CWM help clients minimize their tax liability?

6. What is the difference between a tax deduction and a tax credit?

7. What is the primary goal of wealth transfer strategies?

8. What is the potential downside of relying solely on your employer's life insurance coverage?

9. How can a high net worth individual benefit from international wealth management?

10. What is the purpose of a will and trust in estate planning?

11. What is the key difference between stocks and bonds as investment products?

12. How do real estate investment trusts (REITs) generate income for investors?

13. What is a fiduciary responsibility?

14. What is the main purpose of economic indicators?

15. What is an example of an emerging market?

16. What is the main goal of business succession planning?

17. How can a CWM build and maintain strong relationships with clients?

18. What is the Code of Conduct for a CWM?

19. How can continual education and networking benefit a CWM?

20. What is the primary function of the stock market?

21. What is the main purpose of risk management in wealth management?

22. How can inflation impact investment portfolios?

23. What is the term used to describe the total value of all goods and services produced in a country in a given year?

24. What is a common investment strategy used to reduce risk exposure?

25. What is the purpose of a financial plan?

26. What is a common tax planning strategy used by high net worth individuals?

27. What is the purpose of a trust in estate planning?

28. What is the main purpose of insurance planning?

29. How do foreign exchange markets facilitate global trade?

30. What is a common investment product used to save for retirement?

31. What is the purpose of using tax-efficient investments?

32. How do mutual funds provide diversification to investors?

33. What is the primary goal of capital gains tax?

34. How do exchange-traded funds (ETFs) differ from mutual funds?

35. What is the term used to describe a company's outstanding debt?

36. What is the main goal of foreign exchange market participants?

37. How can trade agreements affect investment decisions?

38. What is an example of a potential conflict of interest for a financial advisor?

39. How can a CWM assist business owners with retirement planning?

40. What is the purpose of using international diversification in investment portfolios?

41. What is one of the key benefits of using a financial advisor?

42. What are some factors that should be considered when determining asset allocation for a client's portfolio?

43. How can a CWM utilize international wealth management for tax planning?

44. How can a CWM help retirees with wealth management?

45. What is the main purpose of a financial plan review?

46. Why should high net worth individuals consider using financial advisors?

47. What is the main difference between a defined contribution plan and a defined benefit plan?

48. What is the purpose of performing a financial analysis for a client?

49. How can a CWM assist with retirement planning for younger clients?

50. How can a CWM address the unique challenges faced by high net worth individuals?

Practice Question Set 3

1. What is the purpose of asset allocation in wealth management?

2. What is the difference between asset allocation and asset classes?

3. What is the role of a financial planner in wealth management?

4. What are some common types of alternative investments?

5. How has technology impacted wealth management?

6. What is the purpose of a systematic withdrawal plan in retirement planning?

7. What is the difference between a Donor-Advised Fund and a Charitable Trust?

8. How can individuals manage their emotions in terms of wealth management?

9. What is the key element in an effective exit planning strategy?

10. What is the Sharpe Ratio used for in evaluating investment performance?

11. What is the most common method of risk management in wealth management?

12. How does a wealth manager help clients in terms of capital preservation?

13. What are some common investment strategies for retirement planning?

14. What are some common types of financial instruments used in wealth management?

15. How does a wealth manager incorporate charitable giving into financial planning?

16. What is the purpose of a systematic investment plan?

17. What are some potential benefits of using a wealth manager?

18. What is a common method for calculating risk tolerance?

19. How can individuals use debt restructuring as an investment strategy?

20. How can individuals use capital raising as an investment strategy?

21. How do hedge funds differ from other types of investments?

22. What are the key elements of a personal financial plan?

23. In what ways does a financial planner consider risk management in wealth management?

24. What is the difference between a defined-benefit and defined-contribution retirement plan?

25. How can individuals use rebalancing strategies to optimize their portfolios?

26. What are some potential drawbacks of private equity investments?

27. How can a wealth manager help with education planning?

28. What are some unconventional solutions for managing financial setbacks?

29. How do investments in real estate typically differ from investments in stocks or bonds?

30. How can individuals use debt consolidation as an investment strategy?

31. How is portfolio diversification different from asset allocation?

32. In what scenarios may long-term care insurance be beneficial for individuals?

33. What is the purpose of benchmarking in performance evaluation?

34. Which type of annuity provides payments for a specific period of time?

35. How can individuals use artificial intelligence in wealth management?

36. What is the difference between a financial planner and a wealth manager?

37. What is the purpose of rebalancing a portfolio?

38. What are some key considerations when evaluating investment performance?

39. What is the role of a Chartered Wealth Manager (CWM)?

40. How can individuals use a systematic investment plan as a wealth management tool?

41. What are some key factors to consider when choosing a financial advisor?

42. What is a common method of managing risk in wealth management?

43. How can individuals use artificial intelligence in wealth management?

44. In what ways can artificial intelligence improve investment decision-making?

45. How can individuals use tax planning as part of wealth management?

46. What strategies can individuals use for retirement planning?

47. What is an uncommon investment strategy that individuals can incorporate into wealth management?

48. What is the purpose of a systematic withdrawal plan in retirement planning?

49. How can individuals use diversification as a risk management strategy?

Practice Question Set 4

1. What is the role of a Chartered Wealth Manager (CWM)?

2. Define wealth management.

3. What is the purpose of a comprehensive financial plan?

4. What are some of the key elements of a successful wealth management strategy?

5. What are some common financial goals that individuals and families may have?

6. What impact can inflation have on wealth?

7. Explain the difference between active and passive investment management.

8. What is asset allocation and why is it important in wealth management?

9. How can a wealth manager assist in tax planning?

10. What is the purpose of risk management in wealth management?

11. How does a wealth manager determine a client's risk tolerance?

12. What is estate planning and why is it important in wealth management?

13. What is the role of a wealth manager in the overall financial planning process?

14. How can a wealth manager assist in philanthropic planning?

15. What factors should be considered when choosing investment strategies for a client's portfolio?

16. How can a wealth manager help clients navigate the complexities of international wealth management?

17. What are some potential challenges in international wealth management?

18. What are some strategies for managing unexpected wealth, such as inheritance or a windfall?

19. How can a wealth manager help in managing financial crises, such as recession or market downturn?

20. What are some trends and innovations currently shaping the field of wealth management?

21. Provide examples of financial goals that may be included in a comprehensive financial plan.

22. What is the difference between monetary assets and real assets?

23. How does diversification help manage risk in an investment portfolio?

24. What is the purpose of a trust in estate planning?

25. Describe the role of a wealth manager in holistic financial planning.

26. How can a wealth manager help clients achieve philanthropic goals while also preserving wealth?

27. How do changes in personal circumstances, such as a job loss or divorce, affect a financial plan?

28. What are some key considerations for managing wealth internationally?

29. What are some potential pitfalls to avoid in wealth management?

30. Discuss the importance of regularly reviewing and updating a financial plan.

31. How can a wealth manager assist in minimizing taxes on a client's wealth?

32. What are some potential risks associated with international wealth management?

33. How can a wealth manager help in developing an effective exit strategy for a business or investment?

34. What are some strategies for managing financial crises, such as bankruptcy?

35. What are some potential challenges facing the future of wealth management?

36. Explain the importance of maintaining a balance between tradition and innovation in wealth management.

37. How can a wealth manager help in managing unexpected wealth, such as an inheritance or windfall?

38. What is the role of a wealth manager in providing guidance during periods of economic downturn?

39. What are the key factors to consider when choosing investment strategies?

40. What is the difference between traditional and online advisory services?

41. Explain the importance of maintaining a diversified investment portfolio.

42. How can a wealth manager help in managing financial risks?

43. What are some potential benefits of international wealth management?

44. Why is proper tax planning an important aspect of wealth management?

45. What are some potential challenges in managing international wealth?

46. What is the role of technology in wealth management?

47. How can a wealth manager assist in developing an exit strategy for a business or investment?

48. What are some potential challenges faced by individuals who experience unexpected increases in wealth?

Practice Exam Questions w/ Answers

Book 1 - Wealth Management Strategies

Practice Question Set 1

1. What are the benefits of pursuing a Chartered Wealth Manager (CWM) designation?

Answer: Some potential benefits include higher job prospects, increased credibility, and potential for higher salary.

2. What is estate planning?

Answer: Estate planning is the process of managing and distributing an individual's assets in a way that aligns with their goals and objectives, while minimizing taxes and potential legal complications.

3. What is the role of a CWM in wealth management?

Answer: A CWM is responsible for creating and implementing strategies to preserve and grow their client's wealth, while also managing risks and minimizing tax liabilities.

4. What is the importance of estate planning?

Answer: Estate planning is important because it allows individuals to have control over how their assets are distributed after their death, while minimizing taxes and potential legal issues.

5. Name three types of clients for wealth management.

Answer: High net worth individuals, business owners, and family offices.

6. What is the Code of Conduct for CWMs?

Answer: The Code of Conduct outlines the ethical and professional standards that CWMs must adhere to in their practice.

7. What is asset allocation?

Answer: Asset allocation is the process of dividing investments among different asset classes, such as stocks, bonds, and real estate, in order to create a diversified portfolio.

8. What is risk management in portfolio management?

Answer: Risk management involves identifying and mitigating potential risks and losses in the investment portfolio.

9. What are the steps of the estate planning process?

Answer: Gathering information, analyzing goals and objectives, and creating a plan.

10. Name three types of taxes that may impact an individual's wealth.

Answer: Income tax, capital gains tax, and estate tax.

11. How can tax efficient investing help minimize tax liability?

Answer: Tax efficient investing involves strategic decisions about when to buy and sell investments in order to minimize the amount of taxes owed.

12. What is the role of client relationship management in wealth management?

Answer: Client relationship management involves building trust, effective communication, and handling difficult situations with clients.

13. Name five common investment vehicles.

Answer: Stocks, bonds, mutual funds, real estate, and alternative investments.

14. What is the difference between a trust and a will?

Answer: A trust allows for the transfer of assets during one's lifetime, while a will dictates the distribution of assets after death.

15. What is the legal framework for estate and trust law?

Answer: The legal framework for estate and trust law includes state laws, federal tax laws, and common law.

16. What is the role of a CWM in tax planning?

Answer: A CWM may provide guidance on tax efficient investment strategies and work with legal experts to create estate plans that minimize tax liabilities.

17. How can a CWM build trust with their clients?

Answer: By being transparent, honest, and acting in the best interest of their clients.

18. What are three types of alternative investments?

Answer: Private equity, hedge funds, and commodities.

19. What is the fiduciary duty of a CWM?

Answer: A fiduciary duty means that a CWM must act in the best interest of their clients and always prioritize their clients' needs above their own.

20. What is the difference between risk tolerance and risk capacity?

Answer: Risk tolerance refers to an individual's ability to handle market fluctuations, while risk capacity refers to their financial ability to sustain losses.

21. What is the purpose of diversification in portfolio management?

Answer: Diversification helps to reduce risk by spreading investments across different asset classes.

22. What are the goals of estate planning?

Answer: The goals of estate planning may include minimizing taxes, ensuring assets are distributed according to one's wishes, and providing financial security for beneficiaries.

23. How can wealth management strategies differ for high net worth individuals compared to other clients?

Answer: High net worth individuals may require more complex and personalized strategies, such as family office services and succession planning.

24. What is an uncommon approach to asset allocation?

Answer: Impact investing, which involves investing in companies or funds that align with one's personal values and beliefs.

25. What is the purpose of tax planning in wealth management?

Answer: The purpose of tax planning is to minimize tax liabilities for individuals and their heirs.

26. How does estate planning address potential legal complications?

Answer: By designating beneficiaries, creating wills and trusts, and establishing powers of attorney.

27. Name three types of risk that investors should consider in portfolio management.

Answer: Market risk, credit risk, and liquidity risk.

28. What is the role of professionalism in the Code of Conduct for CWMs?

Answer: Professionalism is expected in all interactions with clients and requires CWMs to act with honesty, integrity, and respect.

29. How can clients benefit from a CWM's knowledge of alternative investments?

Answer: A CWM can provide access to potentially higher yielding investments and help diversify a portfolio.

30. What is a common tax strategy for minimizing estate taxes?

Answer: Gifting assets during one's lifetime to reduce the overall value of the estate.

31. What are some common ways that individuals can minimize tax liabilities?

Answer: Utilizing tax-deferred retirement accounts, taking advantage of tax deductions and credits, and investing in tax-efficient vehicles.

32. What is a potential risk of investing in alternative investments?

Answer: Alternative investments often have lower liquidity, meaning that they may be difficult to sell quickly.

33. What is the purpose of the estate planning process?

Answer: To create a plan for the preservation and transfer of wealth that aligns with an individual's goals and objectives.

34. Name two benefits of estate planning.

Answer: Ensuring assets are distributed according to one's wishes and minimizing potential legal complications.

35. How can a CWM effectively communicate with clients?

Answer: By actively listening, using clear and concise language, and providing regular updates and reports.

36. What is the role of insurance in wealth management?

Answer: Insurance can be used to mitigate risks and protect assets, such as life insurance for business owners or disability insurance for high net worth individuals.

37. How does tax planning differ from tax preparation?

Answer: Tax planning involves taking strategic actions throughout the year to minimize tax liabilities, while tax preparation is the process of filing taxes.

38. How can a CWM help clients with business succession planning?

Answer: A CWM can assist in creating a plan to ensure a smooth transition of business ownership to the next generation or key employees.

39. Name two strategies for minimizing risk in portfolio management.

Answer: Diversification and asset allocation.

40. What is the importance of staying up-to-date on tax laws and regulations?

Answer: Tax laws and regulations are always changing, so it is important for CWMs to stay current in order to provide the most effective advice for their clients.

41. What is a potential benefit of investing in real estate?

Answer: Real estate can provide both income and potential for appreciation, diversifying a portfolio and providing a hedge against inflation.

42. What is a potential drawback of investing in private equity?

Answer: Private equity often involves high minimum investments and can be highly illiquid, meaning investors may not be able to sell their shares quickly.

43. What is a potential challenge of estate planning for blended families?

Answer: There may be conflicts over who should receive assets and how much, especially if there are children from previous marriages.

44. How can estate planning help avoid potential family conflicts?

Answer: By clearly designating beneficiaries and having open discussions with family members about one's wishes for their assets.

45. How can a CWM assist clients in diversifying their portfolio?

Answer: By analyzing their risk tolerance and identifying appropriate asset classes and investments.

46. What are the potential benefits of investing in alternative investments?

Answer: Potential higher returns and ability to diversify a portfolio.

47. What is a common concern for high net worth individuals when it comes to estate planning?

Answer: Minimizing potential estate taxes that their beneficiaries may owe upon their death.

48. How can a CWM address potential conflicts of interest?

Answer: By being transparent and prioritizing their clients' needs above their own.

49. What is a potential benefit of investing in hedge funds?

Answer: Potential for higher returns and ability to diversify a portfolio.

50. How can CWMs help clients plan for unexpected events, such as disability or long-term care needs?

Answer: By incorporating insurance solutions into their wealth management plan and providing guidance on appropriate savings and investment strategies.

Practice Question Set 2

1. What is the primary purpose of a financial plan?

Answer: The primary purpose of a financial plan is to help individuals or organizations achieve their financial goals and objectives.

2. What are the key components of a financial plan?

Answer: The key components of a financial plan include asset allocation, risk management, tax planning, retirement planning, and estate planning.

3. What is the role of asset allocation in a financial plan?

Answer: Asset allocation is the process of dividing investments across different asset classes to achieve a desired level of return and risk. It plays a critical role in portfolio diversification and risk management.

4. How can risk be managed in a financial plan?

Answer: Risk can be managed in a financial plan through various strategies such as diversification, insurance, and hedging techniques.

5. What are the three types of risk?

Answer: The three types of risk are market risk, credit risk, and liquidity risk.

6. Why is tax planning an important aspect of a financial plan?

Answer: Tax planning helps individuals and organizations reduce their taxable income and maximize their after-tax returns, ultimately helping them achieve their financial goals.

7. What is the purpose of retirement planning?

Answer: Retirement planning is the process of setting financial goals and creating a plan to achieve those goals during retirement. It aims to ensure individuals have enough income to support their desired lifestyle during retirement.

8. What is the primary source of retirement income for most Americans?

Answer: For most Americans, Social Security is the primary source of retirement income.

9. What is an annuity and how does it work?

Answer: An annuity is a contract between an individual and an insurance company. The individual makes a lump sum payment or a series of payments to the insurance company, and in return, the insurance company provides a stream of income for a specified period or for life.

10. What is long-term care insurance and why is it important in retirement planning?

Answer: Long-term care insurance helps cover the costs of long-term care services, such as nursing home care, home health care, and assisted living facilities. It is important in retirement planning because it can protect retirement assets from being depleted by long-term care costs.

11. How can tax planning be integrated into retirement planning?

Answer: Tax planning can be integrated into retirement planning by considering the tax implications of different retirement accounts and developing a strategy to withdraw funds in the most tax-efficient way.

12. What is the goal of estate planning?

Answer: The goal of estate planning is to ensure that a person's assets are transferred to their intended beneficiaries in the most efficient and tax-favorable manner.

13. What is an index fund and how does it work?

Answer: An index fund is a type of mutual fund or exchange-traded fund that tracks a particular market index, such as the S&P 500. It works by investing in a portfolio of stocks that mirror the composition of the chosen index.

14. What are the advantages of passive investing?

Answer: The advantages of passive investing include lower fees, consistent returns, and reduced risk compared to actively managed funds.

15. What is fundamental analysis and how is it used in investment analysis?

Answer: Fundamental analysis is a method of evaluating the value of a security by analyzing its financial and economic factors, such as company financials and competition. It is used in investment analysis to determine whether a security is undervalued, overvalued, or fairly priced.

16. How does technical analysis differ from fundamental analysis?

Answer: Technical analysis involves analyzing past price trends and patterns to predict future price movements, while fundamental analysis focuses on financial and economic factors to determine a security's value.

17. What is a derivative and how is it used in portfolio management?

Answer: A derivative is a financial instrument that derives its value from an underlying asset, such as stocks, bonds, or commodities. It is used in portfolio management as a hedging tool to manage risk or enhance returns.

18. What are some strategies for valuing investments?

Answer: Some strategies for valuing investments include discounted cash flow analysis, price-to-earnings ratio, and market multiples.

19. What is succession planning and why is it important in estate planning for business owners?

Answer: Succession planning involves identifying and developing successors for key leadership positions in a company. It is important in estate planning for business owners to ensure the successful transition of business ownership and leadership to the next generation.

20. What is the purpose of a buy-sell agreement?

Answer: A buy-sell agreement is a legally binding contract that outlines what will happen to a business in the event that a co-owner passes away, becomes disabled, or wants to sell their share of the business.

21. What are the types of insurance that can help manage risks for corporate and executive compensation?

Answer: The types of insurance that can help manage risks for corporate and executive compensation include life insurance, disability insurance, and key person insurance.

22. What are some alternative investments that can potentially provide higher returns but also have higher risks?

Answer: Some alternative investments include hedge funds, private equity, venture capital, and real estate.

23. How can currency risk be managed in global investing?

Answer: Currency risk can be managed in global investing through hedging techniques, such as using currency futures or options, or by investing in currency-hedged funds.

24. What are structured notes and how do they work?

Answer: Structured notes are hybrid securities with features of both debt and equity. They typically offer protection of the principal amount invested while providing a potential return linked to an underlying asset or index.

25. What are the benefits of using structured notes in a portfolio?

Answer: The benefits of using structured notes in a portfolio include diversification, capital protection, and potential for enhanced returns.

26. What are certificates of deposit and how do they work?

Answer: Certificates of deposit (CDs) are a type of financial product offered by banks that pay a fixed interest rate over a specified period of time. They work by depositing a lump sum of money with a bank for a predetermined period, and in return, the bank pays the investor interest and returns the principal amount at the end of the term.

27. What is market risk and how can it be managed?

Answer: Market risk refers to the potential for loss due to changes in market conditions, such as interest rates, inflation, and economic events. It can be managed through diversification, hedging, and asset allocation strategies.

28. What is liquidity risk and how can it be managed?

Answer: Liquidity risk is the risk that an asset cannot be bought or sold quickly enough to prevent a loss. It can be managed by having a mix of liquid and illiquid assets in a portfolio, having a cash reserve, and diversifying across asset classes.

29. What is credit risk and how can it be managed?

Answer: Credit risk is the risk of default on a debt obligation by the issuer. It can be managed by diversifying across issuers and credit ratings and conducting thorough credit analysis.

30. What is family governance and why is it important in estate planning?

Answer: Family governance refers to the systems, processes, and structures that govern the relationships and decision-making within a family. It is important in estate planning to help families navigate potential conflicts and ensure a smooth transfer of wealth to the next generation.

31. How can behavioral biases impact decision-making in investing?

Answer: Behavioral biases, such as overconfidence, herd mentality, and loss aversion, can lead to emotion-based decision-making and cause investors to deviate from their predetermined investment goals and strategies.

32. What are common biases that investors should be aware of?

Answer: Common biases that investors should be aware of include confirmation bias, recency bias, and availability bias.

33. What are some uncommon approaches to advanced retirement strategies?

Answer: Some uncommon approaches to advanced retirement strategies include using Roth IRA conversions, creating a retirement income plan, and incorporating longevity insurance.

34. How can derivatives be used to manage risks in a portfolio?

Answer: Derivatives can be used to manage risks in a portfolio by hedging against unpredictable changes in market conditions, such as interest rates, exchange rates, and commodity prices.

35. What is the difference between single-stock futures and stock options?

Answer: Single-stock futures give investors the right to buy or sell a specific amount of an individual stock at a predetermined price and date, while stock options give investors the right, but not the obligation, to buy or sell a specific amount of an individual stock at a predetermined price and date.

36. Why is it important to consider the tax implications when choosing investments?

Answer: Considering the tax implications when choosing investments can help investors optimize their after-tax return and minimize their tax liability.

37. What is a convertible bond and how is it different from a regular bond?

Answer: A convertible bond is a type of bond that can be converted into a predetermined number of shares of the issuer's common stock. It is different from a regular bond in that it provides investors with the option to convert their bond into equity ownership.

38. How can technical analysis be used to identify potential trading opportunities?

Answer: Technical analysis can be used to identify potential trading opportunities by analyzing price trends, patterns, support and resistance levels, and volume.

39. How can family businesses use succession planning to ensure their continued success?

Answer: Family businesses can use succession planning to identify potential successors and groom them for leadership roles, establish a clear plan for leadership transition, and address potential conflicts and challenges.

40. What are some common strategies for valuing a business?

Answer: Some common strategies for valuing a business include the discounted cash flow method, price-to-earnings ratio, and market-based approach.

41. How can diversity and inclusion help manage risks in corporate leadership?

Answer: Diversity and inclusion in corporate leadership can help manage risks by bringing diverse perspectives and expertise to decision-making, promoting transparency and ethical business practices, and reducing the likelihood of groupthink.

Practice Question Set 3

1. What are the key components of a typical financial plan?

Answer: Cash management, debt management, investment management, risk management, tax planning, estate planning.

2. What are some common indicators used in portfolio performance measurement?

Answer: Benchmarking, tracking error, and risk-adjusted returns.

3. How can a wealth manager help clients with tax planning?

Answer: By utilizing strategies such as tax-loss harvesting, asset location, and minimizing capital gains.

4. What is the purpose of diversification in investment planning?

Answer: To spread risk across different asset classes and reduce the impact of market volatility on a portfolio.

5. What are the potential benefits and risks of real estate investments?

Answer: Benefits include potential for income and appreciation, while risks include illiquidity and concentration in a single asset.

6. What is the importance of setting goals in financial planning?

Answer: Goals provide a clear direction and purpose for the financial plan and help clients make more informed decisions.

7. How can alternative investments, such as private equity, add value to a portfolio?

Answer: They can provide diversification, potential for higher returns, and access to different asset classes.

8. What factors should be considered when creating a legacy plan?

Answer: Family values, mission statements, and next generation involvement.

9. How can hedging be used as a tax planning strategy?

Answer: It can help minimize the impact of market fluctuations on a portfolio and reduce taxes paid on gains.

10. What are the potential risks associated with volatile assets, such as cryptocurrencies?

Answer: High volatility, lack of government regulation, and potential for fraud.

11. How can a private foundation be used as a charitable giving strategy?

Answer: Through the creation of a tax-exempt organization that can distribute funds to other charities.

12. What are some potential benefits of using technology in performance measurement?

Answer: Timely and accurate data, greater efficiency, and the ability to track multiple portfolios.

13. What is the purpose of disaster planning in wealth management?

Answer: To mitigate potential risks and protect financial resources in the event of a disaster.

14. How can understanding investor psychology benefit wealth management practices?

Answer: It can help advisors better understand and address their clients' financial goals, fears, and decision-making processes.

15. How can an investor maximize their business value?

Answer: By implementing strategies such as cost-cutting, improving efficiency, and diversifying products and services.

16. What is the role of asset allocation in retirement investment planning?

Answer: To balance risk and return by diversifying investments across different asset classes based on the client's risk tolerance and time horizon.

17. How can a wealth manager help clients generate income in retirement?

Answer: By providing investment strategies, such as dividend-paying stocks, bonds, and annuities that generate regular income.

18. What are some potential benefits of using mission statements in wealth management?

Answer: They can help align financial decisions with personal values and serve as a guide for financial decision making.

19. How can a donor-advised fund be used for charitable giving?

Answer: It allows donors to make tax-deductible contributions to a fund and then recommend distributions to their preferred charities.

20. What are some potential cybersecurity risks for wealth managers?

Answer: Data breaches, phishing attacks, and malware that can compromise sensitive client information.

21. How can a wealth manager help clients build wealth outside of their business?

Answer: By providing diversified investment strategies, minimizing business risk exposure, and creating a succession plan.

22. How can decision-making be influenced by emotions and biases?

Answer: It can lead to potential misperception of risk and inefficient decision-making.

23. What are some benefits of using goal setting in financial planning?

Answer: It can provide a clear direction and purpose for the financial plan, help clients prioritize their financial goals, and measure progress.

24. How can tracking error measure the performance of a portfolio?

Answer: It calculates the difference between the returns of a portfolio and its benchmark, providing a measure of risk relative to the benchmark.

25. What is the impact of inflation on long-term financial planning?

Answer: It reduces the purchasing power of money and can affect the ability to achieve financial goals.

26. How does estate planning help protect an individual's assets?

Answer: It can help minimize estate taxes, avoid probate, and ensure assets are distributed according to the individual's wishes.

27. What are the potential advantages of investing in commodities?

Answer: Diversification, potential inflation hedge, and global demand for resources.

28. How can rebalancing be used to manage risk in a portfolio?

Answer: By periodically adjusting the portfolio back to its target asset allocation, minimizing exposure to any one asset class.

29. What factors should be considered when selecting a portfolio benchmark?

Answer: Similarity to the portfolio's investment objectives, risk tolerance, and investment strategy.

30. What is the role of risk management in a financial plan?

Answer: To identify potential risks and implement strategies to mitigate or transfer those risks.

31. How can a wealth manager help clients diversify their investments?

Answer: By providing access to different asset classes, such as stocks, bonds, real estate, and alternative investments.

32. What is the role of legacy planning in wealth management?

Answer: To ensure a smooth transfer of assets to the next generation and preserve family wealth for future generations.

33. How can the owner of a privately-held business maximize their wealth?

Answer: By implementing strategies such as increasing efficiency, cost-cutting, and diversifying products and services.

34. What are some potential risks of investing in hedge funds?

Answer: Illiquidity, high fees, and potential underperformance compared to the market.

35. How can legacy planning benefit from the involvement of the next generation?

Answer: They can provide insights on family values and goals, increasing the likelihood of a smooth transfer of wealth.

36. What are some potential benefits of using mission statements in wealth management?

Answer: They can provide a guide for financial decision making and help align financial decisions with personal values.

37. How can a wealth manager help clients manage long-term care considerations?

Answer: By providing investment strategies to generate income for potential long-term care needs and reviewing insurance options.

38. What is the advantage of using a benchmark to measure portfolio performance?

Answer: It provides a benchmark for evaluating investment performance against a standard.

39. How can advanced tax planning techniques, such as charitable trusts, benefit wealth management?

Answer: They can help reduce tax liability while allowing clients to fulfill their charitable giving goals.

40. How can a wealth manager help clients rebalance their portfolio?

Answer: By periodically reviewing the portfolio and making adjustments based on changes in market conditions and the client's goals.

41. What are the benefits of using risk-adjusted returns in performance measurement?

Answer: It provides a measure of return relative to the amount of risk taken, allowing for comparisons between different investment strategies.

42. What is the role of diversification in managing risk in a portfolio?

Answer: To spread risk across different asset classes and reduce the impact of market volatility on a portfolio.

43. How can a wealth manager help clients with hedging strategies?

Answer: By implementing strategies to minimize the effects of market fluctuations on a portfolio and reduce taxes paid on gains.

44. What are the potential benefits and risks of investing in art?

Answer: Benefits include potential for appreciation and diversification, while risks include high transaction costs and lack of liquidity.

45. How can disaster planning help protect a client's wealth?

Answer: By implementing strategies to mitigate potential risks, such as insurance coverage and alternative investment options.

46. What are some common investment strategies used in retirement planning?

Answer: Asset allocation, generating income through investments, and managing long-term care expenses.

47. How can advanced portfolio performance measurement benefit from technology?

Answer: By providing timely and accurate data, increasing efficiency, and tracking multiple portfolios.

48. What are some risks associated with investing in private equity?

Answer: High fees, illiquidity, and potential underperformance compared to public markets.

49. How can goal setting benefit financial planning?

Answer: It provides a clear direction and purpose for the financial plan, helps clients prioritize their financial goals, and measures progress.

50. What is the potential impact of investment decisions on taxes in wealth management?

Answer: It can affect the amount of taxes paid on capital gains, dividends, and income.

Book 2 - Ethical and Regulatory Framework

Practice Question Set 1

1. What is the role of a CWM in the finance industry?

Answer: The role of a CWM is to provide wealth management services to clients, including wealth creation, preservation, and transfer, as well as investment strategies and risk assessment.

2. What are some job opportunities available for a CWM?

Answer: Job opportunities for a CWM include working in private banks, investment firms, wealth management firms, and financial planning agencies.

3. What is the importance of a CWM in the finance industry?

Answer: A CWM is important in the finance industry as they provide essential services for individuals and institutions looking to grow and manage their wealth effectively.

4. How have the landscape and trends in wealth management changed over time?

Answer: The landscape and trends in wealth management have shifted towards a more holistic and comprehensive approach, with a focus on alternative investments, active management, and risk assessment.

5. What is the history of the Chartered Wealth Manager designation?

Answer: The CWM designation was established in 2000 by the American Academy of Financial Management as a globally recognized certification for wealth management professionals.

6. How has the CWM designation grown over the years?

Answer: The CWM designation has grown in popularity and recognition globally, with an increasing number of professionals seeking this certification to enhance their skills and credibility in the finance industry.

7. What are some current trends in wealth management?

Answer: Current trends in wealth management include a shift towards sustainable and socially responsible investments, the rise of robo-advisors, and the incorporation of digital tools and technologies into wealth management services.

8. What are the three key areas of focus in wealth management?

Answer: The three key areas of focus in wealth management are wealth creation, preservation, and transfer.

9. What is the difference between traditional and alternative investments?

Answer: Traditional investments refer to stocks, bonds, and cash, while alternative investments include assets such as real estate, private equity, hedge funds, and commodities.

10. What is the difference between active and passive investment strategies?

Answer: Active investment strategies involve actively managing a portfolio to beat the market, while passive strategies involve investing in market indexes without active management.

11. What are the two main objectives of investing?

Answer: The two main objectives of investing are to achieve growth and generate income.

12. What is risk tolerance in wealth management?

Answer: Risk tolerance refers to an individual's or institution's ability and willingness to take on risk when making investment decisions.

13. How does diversification help in managing risk?

Answer: Diversification involves spreading investments across different assets to reduce risk and protect against market volatility.

14. What are the three main asset classes in portfolio construction?

Answer: The three main asset classes in portfolio construction are stocks, bonds, and cash or cash equivalents.

15. What is an uncommon factor in portfolio construction?

Answer: An uncommon factor in portfolio construction can be the incorporation of alternative investments, such as real estate, hedge funds, or private equity.

16. What is company analysis in investment strategies?

Answer: Company analysis involves evaluating the financial health and performance of individual companies to make investment decisions.

17. What is industry analysis in investment strategies?

Answer: Industry analysis involves assessing the overall performance and trends of a specific industry when making investment decisions.

18. What is macroeconomic analysis in investment strategies?

Answer: Macroeconomic analysis involves considering factors such as economic growth, inflation, and interest rates in the decision-making process for investments.

19. How do these three types of analysis help in uncovering uncommon investment opportunities?

Answer: These types of analysis help to identify and evaluate uncommon factors that may impact a particular investment opportunity, such as industry or economic trends.

20. What are the three stages of fundamental analysis?

Answer: The three stages of fundamental analysis are charting, indicators, and patterns.

21. What is charting in fundamental analysis?

Answer: Charting involves visually representing price trends and patterns of a particular investment over time.

22. Name one technical indicator used in fundamental analysis.

Answer: Moving averages or Relative Strength Index (RSI) are examples of technical indicators used in fundamental analysis.

23. What are patterns in fundamental analysis?

Answer: Patterns refer to specific price movements on a chart that can indicate future price movements.

24. How does behavioral finance explain the impact of psychological biases on wealth management?

Answer: Behavioral finance takes into account how human emotions and biases can influence investment decisions, leading to possible irrational behaviors.

25. What is decision making in behavioral finance?

Answer: In behavioral finance, decision making refers to the process of evaluating and making investment decisions while taking into account psychological biases and other external factors.

26. How can understanding market sentiments help in wealth management?

Answer: Understanding market sentiments, or the overall mood and attitude of investors, can help in predicting market movements and making investment decisions.

27. What is an uncommon knowledge in behavioral finance?

Answer: An uncommon knowledge in behavioral finance is the understanding and application of behavioral economics principles to make more sound and rational investment decisions.

28. Why is goal setting important in wealth management?

Answer: Goal setting helps individuals and institutions identify their financial objectives and create a plan to achieve them.

29. What is budgeting in the context of wealth management?

Answer: Budgeting involves creating and following a financial plan that allocates resources towards meeting financial goals.

30. What is the importance of retirement planning in wealth management?

Answer: Retirement planning is important in wealth management as it helps individuals and institutions save and invest for their future financial security.

31. What is the Chartered Wealth Manager (CWM) certification?

Answer: The Chartered Wealth Manager (CWM) certification is a globally recognized designation for wealth management professionals.

32. Where can a CWM work?

Answer: A CWM can work in private banks, investment firms, wealth management firms, and financial planning agencies.

33. How does the CWM designation benefit professionals in the finance industry?

Answer: The CWM designation enhances the skills and credibility of professionals in the finance industry, making them more competitive in the job market and increasing their earning potential.

34. What is the historical significance of the CWM designation?

Answer: The CWM designation was established in 2000 by the American Academy of Financial Management as a globally recognized certification for wealth management professionals.

35. How has the popularity of the CWM designation changed over the years?

Answer: The CWM designation has become increasingly popular and recognized globally, with more professionals seeking this certification to advance their careers in the finance industry.

36. What is a current trend in wealth management?

Answer: A current trend in wealth management is the incorporation of digital tools and technologies, such as robo-advisors, into wealth management services.

37. What are the three main areas of focus in wealth management?

Answer: The three main areas of focus in wealth management are wealth creation, preservation, and transfer.

38. What is the difference between traditional and alternative investments?

Answer: Traditional investments refer to stocks, bonds, and cash, while alternative investments include assets such as real estate, private equity, hedge funds, and commodities.

39. What is the difference between active and passive investment strategies?

Answer: Active investment strategies involve actively managing a portfolio to beat the market, while passive strategies involve investing in market indexes without active management.

40. What are the two main objectives of investing?

Answer: The two main objectives of investing are to achieve growth and generate income.

41. What is risk tolerance in wealth management?

Answer: Risk tolerance refers to an individual's or institution's ability and willingness to take on risk when making investment decisions.

42. How does diversification help in managing risk?

Answer: Diversification involves spreading investments across different assets to reduce risk and protect against market volatility.

43. What are the three main asset classes in portfolio construction?

Answer: The three main asset classes in portfolio construction are stocks, bonds, and cash or cash equivalents.

44. What is an uncommon factor in portfolio construction?

Answer: An uncommon factor in portfolio construction can be the incorporation of alternative investments, such as real estate, hedge funds, or private equity.

45. What is company analysis in investment strategies?

Answer: Company analysis involves evaluating the financial health and performance of individual companies to make investment decisions.

46. What is industry analysis in investment strategies?

Answer: Industry analysis involves assessing the overall performance and trends of a specific industry when making investment decisions.

47. What is macroeconomic analysis in investment strategies?

Answer: Macroeconomic analysis involves considering factors such as economic growth, inflation, and interest rates in the decision-making process for investments.

48. How do these three types of analysis help in uncovering uncommon investment opportunities?

Answer: These types of analysis help to identify and evaluate uncommon factors that may impact a particular investment opportunity, such as industry or economic trends.

49. What are the three stages of fundamental analysis?

Answer: The three stages of fundamental analysis are charting, indicators, and patterns.

50. What is charting in fundamental analysis?

Answer: Charting involves visually representing price trends and patterns of a particular investment over time.

Practice Question Set 2

1. What is the main objective of wealth management?

Answer: To provide personalized financial strategies to preserve, grow, and transfer wealth.

2. What is the role of a Certified Wealth Manager (CWM) in the field of wealth management?

Answer: A CWM is responsible for developing and implementing tailored financial plans for clients, based on their specific needs, goals, and risk tolerance.

3. What are the three pillars of wealth management?

Answer: Asset management, risk management, and wealth transfer.

4. What are some factors that influence a client's risk tolerance?

Answer: Age, income, investment objectives, and financial goals.

5. How can a CWM help clients minimize their tax liability?

Answer: By implementing tax-efficient investment strategies and utilizing uncommon tax planning methods.

6. What is the difference between a tax deduction and a tax credit?

Answer: A tax deduction reduces taxable income, while a tax credit directly reduces the amount of taxes owed.

7. What is the primary goal of wealth transfer strategies?

Answer: To efficiently transfer assets to future generations while minimizing the impact of taxes.

8. What is the potential downside of relying solely on your employer's life insurance coverage?

Answer: The coverage may not be sufficient for your needs and it may end if you leave the company.

9. How can a high net worth individual benefit from international wealth management?

Answer: It can provide opportunities for diversifying investment portfolios and minimizing tax liabilities.

10. What is the purpose of a will and trust in estate planning?

Answer: To ensure that a person's assets are distributed according to their wishes after their death.

11. What is the key difference between stocks and bonds as investment products?

Answer: Stocks represent ownership in a company, while bonds represent debt owed by a company or government.

12. How do real estate investment trusts (REITs) generate income for investors?

Answer: Through rental income from properties owned by the REIT.

13. What is a fiduciary responsibility?

Answer: The legal obligation of a financial advisor to act in their client's best interests.

14. What is the main purpose of economic indicators?

Answer: To gauge the health and direction of an economy.

15. What is an example of an emerging market?

Answer: Countries with rapidly growing economies such as India, China, and Brazil.

16. What is the main goal of business succession planning?

Answer: To ensure a smooth transfer of ownership and management of a business to the next generation.

17. How can a CWM build and maintain strong relationships with clients?

Answer: By providing exceptional service, personalized attention, and regular communication.

18. What is the Code of Conduct for a CWM?

Answer: A set of ethical standards and guidelines to be followed while providing financial advice to clients.

19. How can continual education and networking benefit a CWM?

Answer: It allows for staying updated on industry changes and trends and for building a professional network for potential clients and referrals.

20. What is the primary function of the stock market?

Answer: To provide a platform for companies to raise capital by selling shares of their ownership.

21. What is the main purpose of risk management in wealth management?

Answer: To protect against potential losses and mitigate risk exposure in an investment portfolio.

22. How can inflation impact investment portfolios?

Answer: Inflation reduces the purchasing power of money and can negatively affect the value of investments.

23. What is the term used to describe the total value of all goods and services produced in a country in a given year?

Answer: Gross Domestic Product (GDP).

24. What is a common investment strategy used to reduce risk exposure?

Answer: Diversification - investing in a variety of assets to minimize the impact of market fluctuations.

25. What is the purpose of a financial plan?

Answer: To provide a roadmap for achieving financial goals and objectives.

26. What is a common tax planning strategy used by high net worth individuals?

Answer: Income shifting - transferring income from one tax bracket to another to reduce overall tax liability.

27. What is the purpose of a trust in estate planning?

Answer: To hold and manage assets for designated beneficiaries, often with tax benefits.

28. What is the main purpose of insurance planning?

Answer: To mitigate financial risk through the use of various types of insurance products.

29. How do foreign exchange markets facilitate global trade?

Answer: By providing a platform for exchanging one currency for another.

30. What is a common investment product used to save for retirement?

Answer: Employer-sponsored 401(k) plans.

31. What is the purpose of using tax-efficient investments?

Answer: To minimize the impact of taxes on investment returns.

32. How do mutual funds provide diversification to investors?

Answer: By pooling money from multiple investors to purchase a variety of assets.

33. What is the primary goal of capital gains tax?

Answer: To tax the profits made from the sale of an asset.

34. How do exchange-traded funds (ETFs) differ from mutual funds?

Answer: ETFs trade like stocks on exchanges and have lower expense ratios compared to mutual funds.

35. What is the term used to describe a company's outstanding debt?

Answer: Bonds.

36. What is the main goal of foreign exchange market participants?

Answer: To buy low and sell high to generate a profit.

37. How can trade agreements affect investment decisions?

Answer: They can impact the cost of imports and exports, which in turn can affect the profitability of companies and investment returns.

38. What is an example of a potential conflict of interest for a financial advisor?

Answer: Receiving a commission for recommending certain investment products.

39. How can a CWM assist business owners with retirement planning?

Answer: By offering employee benefit plans such as 401(k) plans, pension plans, and stock options.

40. What is the purpose of using international diversification in investment portfolios?

Answer: To reduce risk exposure by investing in multiple markets and economies.

41. What is one of the key benefits of using a financial advisor?

Answer: Access to professional expertise and personalized financial advice.

42. What are some factors that should be considered when determining asset allocation for a client's portfolio?

Answer: Risk tolerance, investment objectives, and time horizon.

43. How can a CWM utilize international wealth management for tax planning?

Answer: By utilizing tax treaties and different tax rates in other countries to minimize overall tax liability.

44. How can a CWM help retirees with wealth management?

Answer: By providing strategies for generating income, managing risk, and minimizing taxes in retirement.

45. What is the main purpose of a financial plan review?

Answer: To ensure the financial plan is aligned with the client's goals and objectives and to make adjustments as needed.

46. Why should high net worth individuals consider using financial advisors?

Answer: To properly manage and grow their wealth, minimize tax liability, and obtain specialized advice for complex financial situations.

47. What is the main difference between a defined contribution plan and a defined benefit plan?

Answer: In a defined contribution plan, the amount contributed is defined, while in a defined benefit plan, the benefit amount is defined.

48. What is the purpose of performing a financial analysis for a client?

Answer: To assess their financial health, identify areas for improvement, and develop a plan to achieve financial goals.

49. How can a CWM assist with retirement planning for younger clients?

Answer: By offering advice on starting a retirement savings plan early and making informed investment decisions.

50. How can a CWM address the unique challenges faced by high net worth individuals?

Answer: By providing specialized services such as international wealth management, tax planning, and risk mitigation strategies.

Practice Question Set 3

1. What is the purpose of asset allocation in wealth management?

Answer: The purpose of asset allocation in wealth management is to diversify investments and manage risk.

2. What is the difference between asset allocation and asset classes?

Answer: Asset allocation refers to the overall distribution of an investor's portfolio, while asset classes refer to different types of investments such as stocks, bonds, and real estate.

3. What is the role of a financial planner in wealth management?

Answer: A financial planner can help individuals create a tailored investment plan and provide guidance on managing financial goals, risk tolerance, and time horizon.

4. What are some common types of alternative investments?

Answer: Private equity, hedge funds, and real estate are commonly considered alternative investments.

5. How has technology impacted wealth management?

Answer: Technology has made wealth management more accessible, efficient, and cost-effective with the rise of robo-advisors, digital banking, and artificial intelligence.

6. What is the purpose of a systematic withdrawal plan in retirement planning?

Answer: A systematic withdrawal plan ensures that a retiree has a steady and reliable income stream by withdrawing a fixed amount of money at regular intervals.

7. What is the difference between a Donor-Advised Fund and a Charitable Trust?

Answer: A Donor-Advised Fund is a charitable giving account managed by a public charity, while a Charitable Trust is a legally binding agreement between a donor, trustee, and beneficiary.

8. How can individuals manage their emotions in terms of wealth management?

Answer: Individuals can manage their emotions by recognizing and understanding behavioral biases, learning to control emotional responses, and maintaining a long-term perspective.

9. What is the key element in an effective exit planning strategy?

Answer: Regular rebalancing of investments is a key element in an effective exit planning strategy.

10. What is the Sharpe Ratio used for in evaluating investment performance?

Answer: The Sharpe Ratio is a measure of risk-adjusted return and is used to evaluate the return an investor receives in comparison to the amount of risk taken.

11. What is the most common method of risk management in wealth management?

Answer: Diversification is the most common method of risk management in wealth management.

12. How does a wealth manager help clients in terms of capital preservation?

Answer: Wealth managers can help clients preserve their capital by conducting risk assessments, creating diversified portfolios, and implementing risk management strategies.

13. What are some common investment strategies for retirement planning?

Answer: Annuities, systematic withdrawal plans, and long-term care insurance are common investment strategies for retirement planning.

14. What are some common types of financial instruments used in wealth management?

Answer: Derivatives such as options and futures are commonly used in wealth management to manage risk and enhance returns.

15. How does a wealth manager incorporate charitable giving into financial planning?

Answer: Wealth managers can incorporate charitable giving into financial planning by identifying tax-efficient options, creating donor-advised funds, and incorporating philanthropy into overall financial goals.

16. What is the purpose of a systematic investment plan?

Answer: A systematic investment plan is a way to invest a fixed amount of money regularly over time, reducing the impact of market fluctuations.

17. What are some potential benefits of using a wealth manager?

Answer: Potential benefits of using a wealth manager include professional investment advice, personalized investment strategies, and assistance with risk management and tax planning.

18. What is a common method for calculating risk tolerance?

Answer: A risk tolerance questionnaire is a common method for calculating risk tolerance by assessing individuals' attitudes towards risk.

19. How can individuals use debt restructuring as an investment strategy?

Answer: Individuals can use debt restructuring as an investment strategy to refinance high-interest debt, freeing up cash flow for other investments.

20. How can individuals use capital raising as an investment strategy?

Answer: Individuals can use capital raising as an investment strategy to raise funds for business expansion, new ventures, or other financial goals.

21. How do hedge funds differ from other types of investments?

Answer: Hedge funds typically have less regulations and are only available to accredited investors, with a focus on alternative assets and more risk-seeking strategies.

22. What are the key elements of a personal financial plan?

Answer: A personal financial plan typically includes a statement of financial goals, an analysis of financial resources and liabilities, and a detailed action plan for reaching those goals.

23. In what ways does a financial planner consider risk management in wealth management?

Answer: A financial planner considers risk management in wealth management by analyzing an individual's risk tolerance, diversifying the portfolio, and implementing risk management strategies.

24. What is the difference between a defined-benefit and defined-contribution retirement plan?

Answer: A defined-benefit retirement plan promises a specific payment to the retiree, while a defined-contribution retirement plan depends on the amount of contributions made by the individual.

25. How can individuals use rebalancing strategies to optimize their portfolios?

Answer: Rebalancing strategies can help individuals maintain their target asset allocation and potentially capture gains in certain asset classes while minimizing losses in others.

26. What are some potential drawbacks of private equity investments?

Answer: Private equity investments may have a high barrier to entry, illiquidity, and may be considered high-risk due to the potential for significant returns or losses.

27. How can a wealth manager help with education planning?

Answer: A wealth manager can help with education planning by creating a tailored investment strategy, exploring tax-efficient options, and identifying potential scholarships or financial aid opportunities.

28. What are some unconventional solutions for managing financial setbacks?

Answer: Unconventional solutions for managing financial setbacks may include borrowing from a 401(k) or utilizing a home equity loan.

29. How do investments in real estate typically differ from investments in stocks or bonds?

Answer: Investments in real estate have different risk and return profiles, are less liquid, and have potential for higher potential returns but also higher potential losses compared to stocks or bonds.

30. How can individuals use debt consolidation as an investment strategy?

Answer: Individuals can use debt consolidation as an investment strategy by combining multiple high-interest debts into one lower-interest loan, potentially freeing up cash flow for investing.

31. How is portfolio diversification different from asset allocation?

Answer: Portfolio diversification refers to the variety of investments within an asset class, while asset allocation refers to the distribution of an individual's entire portfolio across different asset classes.

32. In what scenarios may long-term care insurance be beneficial for individuals?

Answer: Long-term care insurance may be beneficial for individuals who anticipate needing long-term care in the future and who want to protect their assets and ensure a level of care they desire.

33. What is the purpose of benchmarking in performance evaluation?

Answer: Benchmarking allows for the comparison of investment performance against a set standard or index to evaluate the effectiveness of investment strategies.

34. Which type of annuity provides payments for a specific period of time?

Answer: A fixed term annuity provides payments for a specific period of time, typically chosen by the individual.

35. How can individuals use artificial intelligence in wealth management?

Answer: Individuals can use artificial intelligence for tasks such as portfolio analysis, risk management, and even investment decision-making.

36. What is the difference between a financial planner and a wealth manager?

Answer: A financial planner typically focuses on creating a tailored financial plan, while a wealth manager focuses on managing and optimizing investments.

37. What is the purpose of rebalancing a portfolio?

Answer: The purpose of rebalancing a portfolio is to maintain the desired target asset allocation and potentially capture gains in certain asset classes while minimizing losses in others.

38. What are some key considerations when evaluating investment performance?

Answer: Some key considerations when evaluating investment performance may include risk-adjusted return, diversification, and benchmarking against industry standards.

39. What is the role of a Chartered Wealth Manager (CWM)?

Answer: A Chartered Wealth Manager (CWM) can provide expertise in wealth management, investment planning, risk management, and solutions for specific financial goals.

40. How can individuals use a systematic investment plan as a wealth management tool?

Answer: Individuals can use a systematic investment plan as a tool to invest over time in a disciplined manner and potentially lessen the impact of market volatility.

41. What are some key factors to consider when choosing a financial advisor?

Answer: Some key factors to consider when choosing a financial advisor may include expertise, certifications, experience, and fees.

42. What is a common method of managing risk in wealth management?

Answer: Diversification is a common method of managing risk in wealth management by investing in a variety of assets to spread out risk.

43. How can individuals use artificial intelligence in wealth management?

Answer: Individuals can use artificial intelligence for tasks such as portfolio analysis, risk management, and even investment decision-making.

44. In what ways can artificial intelligence improve investment decision-making?

Answer: Artificial intelligence can improve investment decision-making by analyzing vast amounts of data and making data-driven decisions, potentially resulting in more efficient and effective investment strategies.

45. How can individuals use tax planning as part of wealth management?

Answer: Individuals can use tax planning as part of wealth management by taking advantage of tax-efficient investment vehicles and strategies, such as tax-loss harvesting.

46. What strategies can individuals use for retirement planning?

Answer: Annuities, long-term care insurance, and systematic withdrawal plans are some common strategies individuals can use for retirement planning.

47. What is an uncommon investment strategy that individuals can incorporate into wealth management?

Answer: Incorporating art into an investment portfolio can be an uncommon but potentially profitable strategy for wealth management.

48. What is the purpose of a systematic withdrawal plan in retirement planning?

Answer: A systematic withdrawal plan ensures that a retiree has a steady and reliable income stream by withdrawing a fixed amount of money at regular intervals.

49. How can individuals use diversification as a risk management strategy?

Answer: Individuals can use diversification by investing in a variety of assets with different levels of risk, potentially lessening the impact of market volatility on their portfolio.

Practice Question Set 4

1. What is the role of a Chartered Wealth Manager (CWM)?

Answer: A CWM is a professional who helps individuals and families manage their financial assets and investments.

2. Define wealth management.

Answer: Wealth management is the professional management of a client's financial assets and investments, including financial planning, investment management, and estate planning.

3. What is the purpose of a comprehensive financial plan?

Answer: A comprehensive financial plan is created to help individuals and families reach their financial goals, manage risks, and make informed decisions about their financial future.

4. What are some of the key elements of a successful wealth management strategy?

Answer: Some key elements include financial planning, investment management, risk management, and tax planning.

5. What are some common financial goals that individuals and families may have?

Answer: Common financial goals include saving for retirement, purchasing a home or vacation property, funding children's education, and protecting assets through estate planning.

6. What impact can inflation have on wealth?

Answer: Inflation can erode the purchasing power of wealth over time, making it important to factor this into financial planning and investment decisions.

7. Explain the difference between active and passive investment management.

Answer: Active investment management involves actively buying and selling securities in an attempt to outperform the market. Passive investment management involves investing in a broad market index to match its performance.

8. What is asset allocation and why is it important in wealth management?

Answer: Asset allocation is the process of dividing a portfolio among different types of assets to achieve a desired level of risk and return. It is important in wealth management because it helps diversify a portfolio and manage risk.

9. How can a wealth manager assist in tax planning?

Answer: A wealth manager can assist in tax planning by identifying tax-efficient investment strategies, coordinating with tax professionals, and minimizing the impact of taxes on a client's wealth.

10. What is the purpose of risk management in wealth management?

Answer: The purpose of risk management in wealth management is to assess potential risks to a client's financial goals and develop strategies to mitigate those risks.

11. How does a wealth manager determine a client's risk tolerance?

Answer: A wealth manager will typically gather information about a client's financial goals, time horizon, and tolerance for potential losses to assess their risk tolerance.

12. What is estate planning and why is it important in wealth management?

Answer: Estate planning involves creating a plan for the distribution of one's assets after their death. It is important in wealth management to ensure that assets are passed on according to a client's wishes and to minimize tax implications.

13. What is the role of a wealth manager in the overall financial planning process?

Answer: The wealth manager plays a vital role in developing and implementing a comprehensive financial plan for their clients, considering various factors such as risk tolerance, tax implications, and estate planning goals.

14. How can a wealth manager assist in philanthropic planning?

Answer: A wealth manager can assist in philanthropic planning by helping clients identify charitable goals and developing a plan to achieve those goals while also considering tax implications and preserving wealth.

15. What factors should be considered when choosing investment strategies for a client's portfolio?

Answer: Factors such as risk tolerance, financial goals, time horizon, and tax considerations should be taken into account when choosing investment strategies for a client's portfolio.

16. How can a wealth manager help clients navigate the complexities of international wealth management?

Answer: A wealth manager can assist clients in understanding tax implications, diversification strategies, and regulatory considerations when managing wealth internationally.

17. What are some potential challenges in international wealth management?

Answer: Some potential challenges include navigating global events, managing risks associated with different currencies and regulations, and staying culturally sensitive.

18. What are some strategies for managing unexpected wealth, such as inheritance or a windfall?

Answer: Strategies may include reassessing financial goals, diversifying investments, and seeking the guidance of a wealth manager.

19. How can a wealth manager help in managing financial crises, such as recession or market downturn?

Answer: A wealth manager can assist by evaluating and adjusting the portfolio, managing risk, and providing support and guidance during uncertain financial times.

20. What are some trends and innovations currently shaping the field of wealth management?

Answer: Trends and innovations include online advisory services, mobile banking, and advancements in cybersecurity to protect clients' wealth.

21. Provide examples of financial goals that may be included in a comprehensive financial plan.

Answer: Examples may include saving for retirement, paying off debt, or purchasing a second home.

22. What is the difference between monetary assets and real assets?

Answer: Monetary assets include cash and financial instruments, while real assets include physical assets such as real estate or commodities.

23. How does diversification help manage risk in an investment portfolio?

Answer: Diversification involves spreading investments across different types of assets, which can help mitigate risk should one asset class perform poorly.

24. What is the purpose of a trust in estate planning?

Answer: A trust is a legal entity that holds assets for the benefit of one or more beneficiaries and can help minimize taxes, avoid probate, and ensure assets are distributed according to a person's wishes.

25. Describe the role of a wealth manager in holistic financial planning.

Answer: A wealth manager takes a comprehensive approach to financial planning, considering various factors such as risk tolerance, tax implications, and estate planning goals, to create a personalized plan for their clients.

26. How can a wealth manager help clients achieve philanthropic goals while also preserving wealth?

Answer: A wealth manager can assist in identifying tax-efficient strategies for charitable giving and ensuring that philanthropic goals align with the overall financial plan.

27. How do changes in personal circumstances, such as a job loss or divorce, affect a financial plan?

Answer: Changes in personal circumstances may require adjustments to the financial plan, such as revisiting financial goals or modifying risk tolerance.

28. What are some key considerations for managing wealth internationally?

Answer: Considerations may include tax implications, regulatory differences, and cultural sensitivities.

29. What are some potential pitfalls to avoid in wealth management?

Answer: Some potential pitfalls include failing to diversify investments, not considering the impact of inflation, and not regularly reviewing and adjusting the financial plan.

30. Discuss the importance of regularly reviewing and updating a financial plan.

Answer: Regularly reviewing and updating a financial plan allows for adjustments to be made to accommodate changing financial goals and personal circumstances, ultimately helping to ensure the plan remains effective.

31. How can a wealth manager assist in minimizing taxes on a client's wealth?

Answer: A wealth manager can help identify tax-efficient investment strategies, coordinate with tax professionals, and evaluate strategies to minimize tax liabilities.

32. What are some potential risks associated with international wealth management?

Answer: Risks may include currency fluctuations, political instability, and regulatory changes.

33. How can a wealth manager help in developing an effective exit strategy for a business or investment?

Answer: A wealth manager can assist in evaluating potential exit strategies, identifying tax implications, and developing a plan that aligns with the client's overall financial goals.

34. What are some strategies for managing financial crises, such as bankruptcy?

Answer: Strategies may include evaluating potential financial options, minimizing expenses, and seeking the guidance of a wealth manager.

35. What are some potential challenges facing the future of wealth management?

Answer: Challenges may include rapidly evolving technology, global events affecting the market, and the need to balance traditional methods with innovation.

36. Explain the importance of maintaining a balance between tradition and innovation in wealth management.

Answer: While innovation can bring about advancements and opportunities, it is important to also consider traditional practices and principles in managing wealth to maintain stability and minimize risk.

37. How can a wealth manager help in managing unexpected wealth, such as an inheritance or windfall?

Answer: A wealth manager can assist by reassessing financial goals, diversifying investments, and developing a plan to preserve and grow the wealth for the long-term.

38. What is the role of a wealth manager in providing guidance during periods of economic downturn?

Answer: A wealth manager can help by evaluating and adjusting the portfolio, managing risk, and providing support and guidance during uncertain financial times.

39. What are the key factors to consider when choosing investment strategies?

Answer: Key factors may include risk tolerance, financial goals, time horizon, and tax implications.

40. What is the difference between traditional and online advisory services?

Answer: Traditional advisory services involve face-to-face consultations with a wealth manager, while online advisory services utilize technology to provide advice and financial planning assistance.

41. Explain the importance of maintaining a diversified investment portfolio.

Answer: Diversification helps to mitigate risk by spreading investments across different asset classes, reducing the impact of poor performance from one particular investment.

42. How can a wealth manager help in managing financial risks?

Answer: A wealth manager can assist in identifying potential risks and developing strategies to mitigate those risks, while also considering factors such as risk tolerance and financial goals.

43. What are some potential benefits of international wealth management?

Answer: Benefits may include accessing new investment opportunities, diversifying assets, and potentially reducing tax liabilities.

44. Why is proper tax planning an important aspect of wealth management?

Answer: Proper tax planning can help minimize the impact of taxes on a client's wealth and ensure that strategies align with their overall financial goals.

45. What are some potential challenges in managing international wealth?

Answer: Challenges may include differences in regulations, currency fluctuations, and managing cultural sensitivities.

46. What is the role of technology in wealth management?

Answer: Technology plays an increasingly important role in wealth management, with advancements in mobile banking, online advisory services, and cybersecurity.

47. How can a wealth manager assist in developing an exit strategy for a business or investment?

Answer: A wealth manager can help evaluate potential exit strategies, identify tax implications, and create a plan that aligns with a client's financial goals.

48. What are some potential challenges faced by individuals who experience unexpected increases in wealth?

Answer: Challenges may include changes in lifestyle, managing family expectations, and navigating potential tax implications.

Printed in Great Britain
by Amazon